Resisting Erasure

Resisting Erasure

Capital, Imperialism, and Race in Palestine

Adam Hanieh
Robert Knox
Rafeef Ziadah

London • New York

First published by Verso 2025
© Adam Hanieh, Robert Knox, Rafeef Ziadah 2025

All rights reserved

The manufacturer's authorized representative in the EU
for product safety (GPSR) is LOGOS EUROPE,
9 rue Nicolas Poussin, 17000, La Rochelle, France
contact@logoseurope.eu

The moral rights of the authors have been asserted

1 3 5 7 9 10 8 6 4 2

Verso
UK: 6 Meard Street, London W1F 0EG
US: 207 32nd Street, New York, NY 10016
versobooks.com

Verso is the imprint of New Left Books

ISBN-13: 978-1-83674-075-9
ISBN-13: 978-1-83674-077-3 (US EBK)
ISBN-13: 978-1-83674-077-3 (UK EBK)

British Library Cataloguing in Publication Data
A catalogue record for this book is available from the British Library

Library of Congress Cataloging-in-Publication Data
Library of Congress Control Number: 2025936352

Typeset in Sabon MT by Hewer Text UK Ltd, Edinburgh
Printed and bound by CPI Group (UK) Ltd, Croydon CR0 4YY

Contents

Acknowledgements   vii

Introduction: Reframing Palestine   1

1. Fossil Capitalism and Empire in the Middle East   19

2. Palestinian Politics and the Oslo Accords   35

3. Racialising Palestine   63

4. Against Normalisation and Erasure   87

Notes   99

Acknowledgements

This pamphlet emerged from a series of educational day schools organised by the group Workers in Palestine in the midst of the genocide in Gaza. Workers in Palestine is a collective formed in response to calls for international solidarity from Palestinian workers and trade unions.

Our deepest gratitude goes to Riya Al'Sanah, a key organiser of the day schools, and all the speakers and activists who helped make these events a success. Many thanks also to Rosie Warren, who encouraged us to transform the talks from the day schools into this text.

The ideas in this pamphlet draw deeply upon discussions with friends and comrades over many years. We hope it stands as a testament to their belief that, even in the darkest of times, we must continue to think, inspire, and act together.

Resisting Erasure

Capital, Imperialism,
and Race in Palestine

Introduction

Reframing Palestine

I grant you refuge in knowing
that the dust will clear,
and they who fell in love and died together
will one day laugh.

Hiba Abu Nada[1]

Since October 2023, Israel's war on Gaza has unfolded with ruthless destruction and human suffering, broadcast to the world in harrowing detail. Entire neighbourhoods reduced to rubble, with residential buildings, hospitals, schools, and vital infrastructure obliterated. The intensity of the bombing has killed tens of thousands of Palestinians, many still missing under the rubble, and left thousands permanently maimed, with amputations performed without anaesthesia in makeshift operating rooms.[2] Gaza now has one of the highest rates of child amputees globally.[3] Israel's blockade of food, water, and medicine has driven Gaza into catastrophic conditions, with famine taking hold across the population. More than a million people have been displaced, sheltering in overcrowded tents amid the ruins of their neighbourhoods, while the psychological toll of unrelenting bombardment and loss is etched into the faces of survivors.

This reality is not the result of an uncontrolled or random act of war but a deliberate policy of destruction. Following the Hamas 7 October attack, Israeli officials openly spoke of their intent to 'flatten' Gaza, and the military strategy has mirrored this rhetoric with brutal precision.[4] The scale of devastation is staggering: cultural landmarks erased, entire families wiped out, and Gaza's healthcare system systematically dismantled through strikes on hospitals, medical personnel, and ambulances. Beyond the immediate violence, Israel's genocide continues a decades-long project of displacing, fragmenting, and erasing Palestinian life – a process that began with the Nakba of 1948, when over 750,000 Palestinians were forcibly expelled from their homes. Today, calls by US President Donald Trump and others to 'relocate' Palestinians to neighbouring Arab states reflect the same objectives of population removal and ethnic cleansing.

But alongside this devastation, we have also witnessed unprecedented worldwide mobilisations in solidarity with Palestine and the people of Gaza. Millions have taken to the streets in the largest global protest movement since the Vietnam War. Encampments have sprung up in universities, and courageous activists have blockaded ports and arms factories. There is now a widespread acknowledgement that a campaign to isolate and divest from Israel is needed more than ever. South

Africa's case against Israel at the International Court of Justice (ICJ) has also carried symbolic weight, highlighting the historical parallels between apartheid in South Africa and Israel's settler-colonial violence, even within the limitations of 'international justice'. The case not only exposed the brutality of Israel's actions, but also the moral bankruptcy of Western states shielding Israel.

The explosive growth of these protest movements and awareness of the Palestinian plight underline a simple truth: for many, the people of Gaza have come to embody the profound injustices of our time. Their struggle for survival pits one of the world's most powerful militaries against a population that has nothing except a desire to be free. This is why Palestine has become a lightning rod for a much deeper rage about the state of the world today. One indication of this is the way that Palestine has *also* become a radicalising impulse for political elites – with parties from the far right through to traditional social democrats (like the Labour Party in Britain) rushing to close ranks behind the Israeli state. Globally, this has involved the repression of protest movements, the criminalisation of activism, and a crackdown on pro-Palestine speech in universities and public spaces.[5] Capitalist states have always worn liberal democracy's velvet glove over a mailed fist – Palestine has brought this reality into sharp relief.

This is a time, in other words, of extreme political polarisation. Yet despite the visceral understanding of what the struggle in Palestine represents, there remain

4 | RESISTING ERASURE

many problems in how it is commonly debated, discussed, and understood.

In the popular media, Palestine is often depicted as a site of timeless conflict fuelled by ancient religious hatreds or competing claims over holy sites. This framing not only distorts history but usually veers into outright racism, portraying Palestinians either as religious fanatics or as a violent mass driven by irrational grievances. A more secular version of this argument renders Israel as a beacon of 'Western democracy' in a region deemed culturally and civilisationally 'backward', with Palestinians recast as little more than anti-semitic aggressors. Such explanations are deeply racist and historically wrong, and fail to provide any meaningful understanding of present-day politics. They serve simply to legitimise and justify Western support for Israel's continuing violence.

A seemingly different perspective is the 'humanitarian' lens, where the focus is placed on the massive levels of Israeli violence and human rights abuses against Palestinians – the bombings, mass arrests, and ongoing dispossession we have witnessed for nearly eight decades. While this framework rightly draws attention to Palestinian suffering, it remains fundamentally inadequate because it cannot explain the persistence of this violence beyond the ideological extremism of Israeli leaders or specific right-wing parties.[6] It fails to account for why this violence is systemic, and why it continues decade after decade regardless of which Israeli party or prime minister is in power.

Humanitarian frameworks also tend to depoliticise the Palestinian struggle, and leave a major question unanswered: why do Western states continue to back Israel unconditionally? And when this problem of Western support is posed, many point to some kind of 'pro-Israel lobby' operating in North America and Western Europe – a false and politically dangerous viewpoint that gets the relationship between Western states and Israel fundamentally wrong.

This humanitarian framing also leads many to turn towards the international legal system as a means to address Israeli human rights violations. Here, the Israeli assault on Gaza is not viewed as a clash of civilisations or religions, but rather one of rights. The problem with this perspective is that, in its appeal to a supposedly universal body of equal rights held by all, international law tends to gloss over the vast asymmetry of power between the Israeli state and the Palestinian people. Politics and power are abstracted, with both 'sides' treated as formally equal bearers of rights. And by ignoring the realities of power – including in the legal system itself – the most powerful are allowed to operate unhindered.

We can see the implications of this in the standards of the international legal regime, which, in its valuing of 'precision' targeting and modern warfare, systematically privileges the military strength of powerful states. The unguided rockets available to Palestinians are inherently 'indiscriminate' and thus illegal, but the highly destructive weaponry of the Israeli state can kill swaths of Palestinian civilians, provided it is deemed 'proportionate'.[7] In this way, the formal equality of the legal argument acts to serve the most powerful – it backgrounds the inequality between the Israeli state and Palestinians, and upholds standards that absolutely protect Israelis while transforming Palestinian lives into collateral damage to be balanced against 'military advantage'.

None of these widespread narratives about Palestine – whether it be the clash of religions, the humanitarian focus on suffering, or the legalist appeal to rights – can explain the persistence of Israeli violence or the unstinting Western support in financing, arming, and legitimating the Israeli state. By depoliticising the Palestinian struggle, they typically ignore the continuities between moments of so-called calm and those of extreme violence (such as the last eighteen months). They also tend to narrow our analytical attention to simply what is going on inside Palestine itself – obscuring the essential link between the dispossession and fracturing of Palestinian society and the dynamics of the wider Middle East region.

Importantly, such perspectives are not exclusively held by those opposed or indifferent to Palestine; they can also surface, albeit inadvertently, among those seeking to act in solidarity.

At times, an insistence on the solely exterminatory character of Israeli state policy is coupled with a focus that merely highlights the 'heroism' and 'resilience' of the Palestinian people. While the struggle for Palestinian liberation has undoubtedly been a heroic one, reducing matters exclusively to this reproduces, in reverse, Orientalising and racialised narratives. The risk here is of attributing almost magical powers to Palestinians, and homogenising Palestinian society. We lose a sense of the political and class differences that exist within Palestine.

This short text presents an alternative perspective. Our goal is not to recount the litany of Israeli violence and the enormous suffering of the people of Gaza since October 2023, or to provide a comprehensive history of Palestine. Many important works have already documented the history, hardships and pitfalls of the Palestinian struggle, and no brief pamphlet can do justice to the full complexity of the Palestinian experience. Instead, our goal is to present some longer-term perspectives that underlie the present situation, and to explore the bigger social forces that have brought us to where we are today. As such, we seek to make a modest contribution to correcting some of the mainstream narratives that are both ahistorical and essentialising. We hope to de-exceptionalise the question of Palestine.

Israel as a Settler-Colonial State

With Israel's establishment in 1948, approximately three-quarters of the original Palestinian population were forcibly displaced from their lands. The expulsions had already begun in 1947, and by the time the state was declared, around 500 Palestinian villages had been

8 | RESISTING ERASURE

destroyed, leaving the majority of Palestinians as refugees scattered in camps across the West Bank, Gaza Strip, and neighbouring countries. Those Palestinians who remained in what became Israel were granted Israeli citizenship, becoming an exploited minority in a state that contradictorily defined itself as 'Jewish and democratic'.[8]

In 1967, the Israeli state occupied another set of Palestinian territories, the West Bank and Gaza Strip. In these newly conquered areas, Palestinians were not given Israeli citizenship, but instead lived under Israeli military occupation. A key part of Israel's control over these occupied territories was the settling of Israeli citizens in militarised towns and neighbourhoods, known as settlements, located in strategic areas between Palestinian cities and villages.

As many have pointed out, these successive waves of colonisation and dispossession fit the classic definition of a settler colony: a territory where foreign populations settle and attempt to displace native inhabitants to establish a new society.[9] However, while the term settler colonialism is now widespread in the scholarship on Palestine, it is often used simply in a descriptive sense. One of our arguments in this text is that for settler colonialism to have analytical strength, it must be framed as one form of the broader expansion of European capitalism. And *because* this kind of colonialism was capitalist, settler colonies were also necessarily bound up with processes of class formation: the production of new classes of capital and labour in the colonised territories.

How this occurred has always been historically specific, taking varying paths across the world. But viewing settler colonialism from this perspective highlights both the continuities and differences between Palestine and other global contexts.

Capital and Labour Under Settler Colonialism

From its inception, capitalism has been international. The ceaseless drive towards expansion, and the necessity to acquire raw materials and energy, meant going beyond domestic territorial boundaries. Through the nineteenth and early twentieth centuries, this expansion was driven by the rivalries of European powers, especially Britain and France, whose conquest of overseas territories was managed under a system of colonial rule.

The Ghanaian anti-colonial leader Kwame Nkrumah put it this way: colonialism 'is that aspect of imperialism which in a territory with an alien government, that government controls the social, economic and political life of the people it governs'.[10] What marks this kind of direct colonialism is the manner in which the rule of capitalism was exercised. The state was directly controlled by the colonial power and supported the activities of foreign capital, breaking up earlier forms of pre-capitalist social life, dispossessing populations from their land, and creating a new workforce and new markets.[11] Through this direct control, European states were also able to exclude the entry of rival capitalist powers, insisting on the exclusive use of their currency

10 | RESISTING ERASURE

(such as British Sterling) and tying all industrial and commercial development to the metropole.

Generally speaking, this model of accumulation held back the emergence of a large-scale capitalist class drawn from the local colonised population. Instead, colonised elites – often mapped onto particular religious or ethnic identities – functioned as local intermediaries for foreign rule, granted privileges in return for ensuring imperial dominance.

In contrast, a different logic took hold in settler-colonial societies (such as the US, Canada, Australia, New Zealand, South Africa – and Israel). Here, European settlers did not merely seek to govern and extract wealth from an existing population, but to dispossess and replace indigenous peoples, reshaping property relations in the process.

Accordingly, settler-colonial capitalism had a different relationship to labour than that found in direct colonies. While some settler societies, like South Africa, relied heavily on the exploitation of indigenous labour, all were also fundamentally driven by the imperative to eliminate, marginalise, or displace the populations already present. This gave settler colonialism a pronounced exterminist character, sometimes manifesting in outright attempts to eradicate and supplant indigenous peoples, as seen in the United States and Australia.

Having marginalised indigenous populations, settler societies thus always needed a non-native, settler working class – one that derived substantial economic and political advantages from the dispossession of the original inhabitants. As a result, this class was typically deeply invested in the survival of settler-colonial capitalism. Such working-class subjectivity was reflected ideologically in heavily racialised and militarised ways of thinking, which simultaneously claimed fealty to defending 'the rights of [settler] labour'. This dynamic explains why explicitly racist labour movements have often been politically dominant in settler colonies, as seen in Israel and Australia.[12]

Alongside these specific characteristics of labour, settler colonies have also tended to foster the growth of their own local capitalist classes. Although frequently these classes maintained links with, or were based in, the metropole, the trajectory of settler societies has often fostered the emergence of distinct capitalist formations and eventual political separation.[13] Despite this separation, however, settler colonies usually remained closely allied to their original metropole, often serving as outposts for the projection of imperial power in their surrounding neighbourhoods (as in Australia).

After the Second World War, a wave of anti-colonial struggles led to the formal dissolution of European empires, and many countries long subjected to colonial rule secured their independence. Yet, this anti-colonial moment unfolded alongside a deeper restructuring of global capitalism. The retreat of Britain, France, and other European powers did not mark the end of imperial domination but rather its reconfiguration, as the United States emerged as the principal force in shaping the world economy. In displacing European hegemony,

American capital and the American state extended its reach through new mechanisms of financial and military dominance, ensuring that the end of direct colonial rule did not signal the end of imperial control.

A fundamental aspect to this restructuring of postwar capitalism was the rise of oil as the dominant fossil fuel, binding the expansion of American power to a new global energy order that we can describe as fossil capitalism. This shift repositioned the Middle East as a vital site of energy extraction while also making it a key battleground of anti-colonial struggle, where fights over sovereignty and resources were shaped by the imperatives of imperial control. In the following chapter we show how Israel played a crucial role in these struggles, its settler-colonial foundations becoming indispensable to a new regional order structured around American dominance.

Anti-Palestinian Racism

Too often, these class dynamics of settler colonialism are ignored – especially in the case of Palestine. Palestinian society, with all its class and political complexities, is flattened into a single undifferentiated mass. Later chapters discuss the differential trajectories of Palestinian labour and capital, and the ways these have been shaped through their incorporation into Israeli settler-colonial capitalism over the past decades. These patterns of class formation have had a profound impact on Palestinian society and politics.

REFRAMING PALESTINE | 13

But closely associated with this is the indelible link between settler colonialism and the ideologies and practices of racism and racial oppression. One of our goals is to show how these ideas of race play out in the context of Palestine, and their enduring centrality to the realities of Israeli settler colonialism.

Our approach to the nature and role of anti-Palestinian racism draws from a rich body of Marxist and anti-colonial thought,[14] which challenges the notion that race is a natural or inherent category.[15] Rather, the opposite is true: 'race' is produced *through racism*. That is to say, in order to marginalise, oppress, and exploit particular groups of people, specific differences – real or imagined – are abstracted and said to be the main characteristic of each member of the group (skin colour, culture, etc.). These differences allow groups to be compared and placed in a hierarchy which in part determines (and justifies) their treatment.[16]

In this way, we can speak of 'racialisation' – the process through which certain arbitrary differences are solidified and abstracted into race. However, while many human societies have marked out difference, they have not all done so in such systematic and globe-spanning ways as capitalism. In Walter Rodney's formulation: 'the white racism which came to pervade the world was an integral part of the capitalist mode of production.'[17]

When European capitalists initially advanced out into the world, they came into contact with non-European, non-capitalist societies. Such societies were destined for plunder and transformation, and this was expressed in racial terms. The 'difference' between non-European and European peoples meant that the 'racially backwards' non-European peoples were ripe for conquest: and the conquerors were to civilise them, by right of their racial superiority.[18]

In this way, some of the core institutions of contemporary capitalism were forged and shaped through a racialised confrontation with the rest of the world. As more and more of the world was brought under the aegis of capitalism, these racialised practices were systematised, and became vital to protecting the interests of powerful capitalist states. In short, actually-existing capitalism is inconceivable without racism and vice versa.[19]

As we discuss in Chapter 3, it is essential to centre this question of race in the case of Palestine, as it underscores the fundamental role of anti-Palestinian racism in sustaining Israeli settler-colonial capitalism. This form of racism renders Palestinians non-human, marking them as inherently disposable and legitimising extreme violence against them. It is this dehumanisation that enables ordinary Israeli citizens to accept, and participate in, the brutal subjugation of Gaza's population. Such racism is not confined to the Israeli right but pervades so-called liberal circles as well – those who may be for 'peace' and oppose specific acts of state violence, yet refuse to confront the fact that the Israeli state itself is structurally founded on the continuing destruction of Palestinian society. Israeli settler colonialism is inseparable from anti-Palestinian racism; it does not merely accompany it but is constitutive of it.

This racialisation of Palestinians is not limited to domestic Israeli society – it operates on a global scale, intersecting with and reinforcing other forms of anti-Arab, anti-migrant, and anti-Muslim racism. Just as anti-Palestinian racism enables unrelenting violence against Palestinians in Gaza, it also serves to legitimise and sustain Western support for the Israeli state at the international level. And critically, this logic of racial dehumanisation persists beyond moments of overt military aggression. One need only look at the casual, almost bureaucratic manner in which the mass expulsion of Palestinians to Egypt and Jordan is now being discussed – a stark illustration of how profoundly normalised this racism has become.

Building Solidarity

Our argument starts with the insistence that Palestine needs to be grounded in an understanding of the Middle East and its place in an oil-centred global capitalism. The structures that sustain Israel's domination over Palestinians are deeply embedded in this wider regional and global order, which has been shaped predominantly by American hegemony since the 1960s. American power in the Middle East has manifested itself through direct military intervention, the actions of international financial institutions, and unwavering Western support for authoritarian regimes across the region. Within this, Israel has played a pivotal part.

Framing Palestine through this regional lens helps clarify why the US and other Western states have extended such unequivocal support – both rhetorical and material – to Israel for so many decades. As we aim to show, this support is not the result of shared 'Western values' or of an Israel 'lobby' that acts to determine US policy in the region. Rather, it is inseparable from the strategic significance of the Middle East region to global capitalism.

This perspective directly links the liberation of Palestine to other struggles in the region (such as in Sudan and Yemen). We mean this not as an analogy or in a moralistic sense, but rather in a real and substantive way. All of these struggles are products of precisely the same social forces, regionally and globally. Such an approach also means rejecting the cynical manipulation of 'anti-imperialist' and pro-Palestine rhetoric by regional capitalist governments who seek to legitimise their own rule. Genuine solidarity lies with the struggles of the people, not with the regimes that suppress them. Solidarity is not an act of charity – but a shared fight against the common structures that produce dispossession, repression, and exploitation across the region and beyond.

At the heart of all of this is the place of the Middle East in the emergence and enduring realities of fossil capitalism. In the following chapter we discuss how the region came to form such a major pivot to oil's rise as the world's principal fossil fuel during the middle of the twentieth century. It was in this context that Israel was established as a settler colony founded on the expulsion of the majority of the Palestinian population in 1947–48. From this moment on, Israeli settler colonialism has bolstered Western imperial interests in the Middle East, especially those of the US. Israel's relationship to the US is deeply connected to the other leading pillar of American power in the region: the oil-rich Gulf Arab monarchies, first and foremost Saudi Arabia. Approaching Palestine in this manner helps to explain the specificities of imperialism and settler colonialism in the Middle East. This is not an abstract exercise – it is key to grasping why Israel exists in its current form, why it continues to receive unwavering Western backing, and why the question of Palestine sits at the leading edge of struggles against fossil capitalism today.

1

Fossil Capitalism and Empire in the Middle East

Palestine is a microcosm of the world: wretched, raging, fraught, and fragmented. On fire. Stubborn. Ineligible. Dignified.

Mohammed El-Kurd, *Perfect Victims: And the Politics of Appeal*

Two primary shifts defined world capitalism in the wake of the Second World War.[1] The first of these was a revolution in the world's energy systems: the emergence of oil as the world's principal fossil fuel, displacing coal and other energy sources across the leading industrialised economies. This fossil fuel transition occurred first in the US, where the consumption of oil surpassed coal in 1950, followed by Western Europe and Japan in the 1960s. Across the wealthy countries represented in the Organisation for Economic Co-operation and Development (OECD), oil made up less than 28 per cent of total fossil fuel consumption in 1950; by the end of

20 | RESISTING ERASURE

the 1960s, it held a majority share. With its greater energy density, chemical flexibility, and easy transportability, oil powered a booming post-war capitalism – enabling the expansion of a range of new technologies, industries, and infrastructure. Liquid fuels derived from oil also moved to the centre of modern war-making: the air, naval, and motorised vehicles that so greatly amplified the destructive power of the Second World War depended on ever-increasing supplies of petroleum.

The global shift to oil did not mean that coal was no longer consumed, or even that there was an overall decline in its use (in fact, coal consumption reached record levels in 2024). Rather, across this period, 'oil-fueled accumulation ... was superimposed on coal-based accumulation'.[2] Overall, the addition of oil to the world's energy matrix led to a doubling of global fossil fuel consumption between 1950 and 1965.[3] This was the beginning of what scientists would later describe as the 'Great Acceleration' – a massive and continued expansion of fossil fuel use that has led inexorably to today's climate emergency.

This global transition to oil was closely connected to a second major post-war transformation: the consolidation of the US as the leading economic and political power. The economic rise of the US had begun in the early decades of the twentieth century, but it was the Second World War that marked the definitive emergence of the US as the most dynamic force in global capitalism, rivalled only by the Soviet Union and its allied bloc. American power arose on the back of the destruction

FOSSIL CAPITALISM AND EMPIRE IN THE MIDDLE EAST | 21

across Western Europe during the war, coupled with the weakening of European colonial rule. As Britain and France faltered, the US took the lead in shaping the architecture of post-war politics and economics, including a new global financial system centred on the US dollar. By the mid-1950s, the US held a 60 per cent share of world manufacturing output and just over a quarter of global GDP – and forty-two of the top fifty industrial corporations in the world were American.[4]

These dual transitions – the rise of an oil-fuelled capitalism and the ascent of American power – had profound implications for the Middle East. The region was essential to the global shift to oil, holding nearly 40 per cent of the world's proven reserves by the mid-1950s.[5] Its oil fields were not only vast but also carried other advantages: production costs were lower than anywhere else in the world, and the region's proximity to Europe made transportation far cheaper than alternative sources. This allowed Middle Eastern oil to enter European markets at prices lower than coal, while US oil producers remained shielded from the pressures of rising European demand. The realignment of Europe's energy supply around the Middle East was swift: between 1947 and 1960, the region's share of Europe's oil imports surged from 43 to 85 per cent.[6] This influx of cheap oil underpinned the rise of new industries – most notably petrochemicals – and transformed transport, infrastructure, and military power. Without the Middle East, Western Europe's oil transition might not have occurred at all.

22 | RESISTING ERASURE

At the time, the enormous oil reserves of the Middle East were concentrated in the Gulf – Saudi Arabia and the smaller Gulf monarchies, as well as Iran and Iraq. Through the first half of the twentieth century, these countries had been ruled by autocratic monarchies supported by the British (except for Saudi Arabia, which was nominally independent of British colonialism). Control over oil production lay firmly in the hands of a few Western oil firms, which paid rents and royalties to these rulers in exchange for extraction rights. These firms were not mere producers; they were giant vertically integrated companies, overseeing every stage of oil's global circulation – from extraction to refining, shipping, and distribution. Their power was unparalleled, shaping not only the energy markets but also the politics of the region. The concentration of ownership in the oil industry far surpassed that of any other sector. By the end of the Second World War, more than 80 per cent of all known oil reserves outside the US and USSR were controlled by just seven Western corporations – infamously known as the 'Seven Sisters'.[7]

The Anti-Colonial Revolt

Despite their apparent unassailable control of world oil, the Seven Sisters were confronted with substantial challenges as the Middle East moved to the centre of world oil markets through the 1950s and 1960s. Across the region, nationalist, communist, and other left-wing movements challenged rulers who had long been backed by British and French colonialism, calling into question the Western-centred regional order. A key fulcrum of these revolts was Egypt, where the British-supported monarch, King Farouk, was toppled by a military coup in 1952 led by a popular military officer, Gamal Abdel Nasser. Nasser forced the withdrawal of British troops from Egypt and paved the way for independence in neighbouring Sudan in 1956. Egypt's sovereignty was crowned with the nationalisation of the British/French-controlled Suez Canal in 1956 – an action celebrated by millions of people across the entire Middle East, and which was met with a failed invasion of Egypt by Britain, France, and Israel. Egypt's break with colonialism helped inspire other movements in neighbouring countries, including Algeria, where a guerrilla war against French occupation began in 1954.

These struggles for national liberation in the Middle East were part of a bigger global post-war revolt that spanned Africa, Asia, and Latin America. Although it is not well recognised today, anti-colonial sentiments were also deeply felt across the oil-rich Gulf states. In Saudi Arabia and the smaller Gulf monarchies, popular support for Nasser ran high, and various left-wing movements protested the corruption, greed, and pro-Western alignment of the ruling families. These struggles highlighted the vulnerability of Gulf monarchs and showed the potential for challenging the control of Middle East oil by Western firms. Indeed, a major factor behind Nasser's regional appeal was his view of oil as 'an inalienable Arab right' that could be used to unify the Arab world against imperialism. In neighbouring Iran, for instance, a popular leader, Mohammad Mossadegh, had come to power in 1951. One of his initial acts was to take over the British-controlled Anglo-Iranian Oil Company (the forerunner of today's BP) in the first oil nationalisation in the Middle East. This nationalisation resonated strongly in nearby Arab states, where the slogan 'Arab oil for the Arabs' captured the growing desire for control over national resources amid a broader anti-colonial wave.[8]

In response to Mossadegh's actions, US and British intelligence officials orchestrated a coup in Iran in 1953, bringing to power a pro-Western government loyal to the Iranian monarch, Mohammad Reza Shah Pahlavi. This was the beginning of a counter-revolutionary wave directed against radical and nationalist movements across the Middle East. The 1953 coup also highlighted a decisive shift in the regional order: while Britain played an important role in the coup, it was the US that led its planning and operation. This was the first time the US government had deposed a foreign ruler during peacetime, and the CIA's involvement in the coup was an important precursor of later US interventions, such as the 1954 coup in Guatemala and the overthrow of Chile's Salvador Allende in 1973.

This more active role for the US in the Middle East was codified in 1957, when President Dwight Eisenhower elaborated the so-called Eisenhower Doctrine as part of his 'Special Message to the Congress on the Situation in the Middle East'.[9] Denouncing 'international communism', Eisenhower guaranteed US readiness 'to employ the armed forces of the United States to assist to defend the territorial integrity and the political independence of any nation in the area'. Although Eisenhower's speech was framed by the supposed Soviet threat, much of what he said addressed events in Egypt, particularly the 1956 nationalisation of the Suez Canal. Eisenhower noted that the canal 'enables the nations of Asia and Europe to carry on the commerce that is essential if these countries are to maintain well-rounded and prosperous economies', and that the Middle East was a 'gateway between Eurasia and Africa . . . [with] about two-thirds of the presently known oil deposits of the world . . . The nations of Europe are peculiarly dependent upon this supply, and this dependency relates to transportation as well as to production.'

Israel and the Significance of Settler Colonialism

It was in this context that Israel emerged as the chief bulwark of American interests in the Middle East. Britain had been the principal backer of the Zionist movement in the early years of the twentieth century, and after Israel's establishment in 1948, it initially remained the foremost ally of the Zionist state-building project. But as the US supplanted European colonial dominance in the Middle East during the post-war period, American support for Israel emerged as the lynchpin of a new regional security order.

26 | RESISTING ERASURE

The key turning point was the 1967 war between Israel and leading Arab states, which saw the Israeli military destroy the Egyptian and Syrian air forces and occupy the West Bank and Gaza Strip, the (Egyptian) Sinai Peninsula, and the (Syrian) Golan Heights. Israel's victory shattered the notions of Arab unity, national independence, and anti-colonial resistance that had crystallised most sharply in Nasser's Egypt. In Egypt, Israel's victory was symbolically reinforced by Nasser's death in 1970 and the coming to power of Anwar Sadat, who subsequently moved to reverse many of Nasser's policies. While popular struggles continued to rock the Middle East after the war – notably in North and South Yemen, Libya, and the Dhofar province of Oman – any political vision that looked to a region-wide transformation became much more distant.

The 1967 war demonstrated that Israel was a powerful force that could be mobilised against any threats to American interests in the region. From that moment onwards, the US pivoted towards Israel, replacing Britain as the country's primary patron. The US began to supply Israel annually with billions of dollars' worth of military hardware and financial support, which has continued through to today. This is why Israel, despite being the world's fourteenth-wealthiest economy by GDP per capita in 2023 – richer than the UK, Germany, or Japan – has received more cumulative US foreign aid than any other country. Indeed, in 2021, before the current genocide began, Israel received more US foreign military financing than *the entire rest of the world combined.*[10]

FOSSIL CAPITALISM AND EMPIRE IN THE MIDDLE EAST | 27

But military aid is only part of the picture. The US provides Israel with billions in loan guarantees, allowing the Israeli state to borrow more cheaply on the world market – one of only six countries to receive such privileges from the US in the past decade.[11] And as the past eighteen months have shown, American support goes far beyond weapons and money. The US serves as Israel's ultimate political shield, blocking accountability and ensuring its impunity on the world stage. This US support to Israel is not tied to one particular president or party – it is bipartisan and permanent.

However, there is a dimension to this US support that often goes unremarked: Israel's special place in underwriting American power is directly connected to its internal character as a settler colony, one founded on an unremitting process of uprooting and expulsion (of which the war against Gaza is the latest manifestation). As we discuss further in Chapter 3, settler colonies must continually work to fortify structures of racial oppression, class exploitation, and dispossession. They are thus typically highly militarised and violent societies, which tend to be reliant upon external support in order to maintain their material privileges in a hostile regional environment. In such societies, a substantial proportion of the population benefits from the oppression of indigenous peoples and comes to understand its privileges in racialised and militaristic terms. For this reason, settler colonies are much more dependable partners of Western imperial interests than 'normal' client states. In the Middle East, for instance, Arab governments supported by the US (such as today's Egypt, Jordan, and Morocco) face repeated challenges from political movements within their own borders and are always forced to accommodate and respond to pressures coming from below. This is different from Israel, where the majority of the population views their interests and privileges as dependent upon continued outside support. This is why British colonialism supported Zionism as a political movement in the early twentieth century – and why the US embraced Israel in the post-1967 moment.

Of course, this does not mean that the US 'controls' Israel, or that there are never differences of opinion between the US and Israeli governments over how this relationship should be sustained. But Israel's ability to maintain a permanent state of war, occupation, and oppression would be deeply imperilled (both materially and politically) without continuous American backing. In return, Israel serves as a loyal partner and safeguard against any threats to American interests in the region. And this extends far beyond the Middle East; Israel has acted globally in supporting repressive US-backed regimes across the world – from apartheid South Africa through to military dictatorships in Latin America.[12]

Alexander Haig, US secretary of state under Ronald Reagan, once put it bluntly: 'Israel is the largest American aircraft carrier in the world that cannot be sunk, does not carry even one American soldier, and is located in a critical region for American national security.' Or, as the former US President Joe Biden stated in

1986: '[Israel] is the best $3 billion investment we make. Were there not an Israel, the United States of America would have to invent an Israel to protect her interests in the region.' True to these words, the US has consistently enabled Israel to act with impunity: since 1945, more than half of all UN Security Council resolutions that the US has vetoed have been those critical of Israel.[13]

The connection between the internal character of the Israeli state and its special place in American power is akin to the role that South African apartheid played for Western imperialism across the African continent. There are important differences between apartheid South Africa and the Israeli state – not least the fact that South Africa's black population made up a majority of the country's working class (unlike Palestinians in Israel) – but as settler colonies, both countries came to act as core organising centres of Western power in their respective neighbourhoods.

Indeed, if we examine the history of Western support for South African apartheid, we see the same sorts of justifications that we see today in the case of Israel (and the same kinds of attempts to block international sanctions and criminalise protest movements). These parallels extend to the role of specific individuals. One little-known example of this is a trip made by a young member of Britain's Conservative Party to South Africa in 1989, during which he argued against international sanctions on South Africa and made the case for why Britain should continue to support the apartheid regime.[14] Decades later, that young Tory, David Cameron, would hold the position of UK foreign minister – and through 2023 become one of the leading cheerleaders of Israel's genocide in Gaza.

The Middle East's centrality to the global oil economy gives Israel a more pronounced place in imperial power than was held by apartheid South Africa. But both cases demonstrate why it is so important to think about how regional and global factors intersect with the internal class and racial features of settler colonies.

This approach helps us understand why arguments that posit an 'Israel lobby' as the explanation for Western support of Israel are wrong. The Lobby argument is essentially a liberal one, which looks to the actions of an 'interest group' to explain how states decide policy, rather than approaching state institutions through their place in capitalism. Of course, this is not to say that there are no pro-Israel organisations that coordinate and lobby around policy. But these organisations – rather than the reason for Western support for Israel – are better thought of as a disciplining mechanism used to police and repress political movements (and speech) on Palestine. Domestically, they help articulate, legitimate, and sustain Western foreign policy in the Middle East, with their influence becoming especially pronounced in moments of growing popular sympathy with the Palestinian struggle. And as we explore in Chapter 3, they also form a key route through which anti-Palestinian racism is promoted and normalised.

Looking Forward: Israel's Economic Integration into the Middle East

The Middle East became even more significant to American global power following the establishment of the Organization of the Petroleum Exporting Countries (OPEC) in 1960 and the nationalisation of crude oil reserves across most of the region (and elsewhere globally) during the 1970s and 1980s. Nationalisation ended the longstanding direct control by Western oil firms of Middle East crude supplies (although American and European firms continued to control most of the global refining, transport, and sale of this oil).[15] In this context, US interests in the region revolved around guaranteeing the stable supply of oil to the world market – denominated in US dollars – and ensuring that oil would not be used as a 'weapon' to destabilise the American-centred global system. Moreover, with Gulf oil producers now earning trillions through the export of crude, the US was also deeply concerned about how these so-called petrodollars circulated through the global financial system – a matter that remains directly consequential to the dominance of the US dollar.[16]

In pursuing these interests, US strategy became fully focused on the survival of the Gulf ruling monarchies, led by Saudi Arabia, as key regional allies. This was particularly important following the overthrow, in 1979, of Iran's Pahlavi dynasty, which had been another mainstay of American interests in the Gulf since the 1953 coup. US support to the Gulf monarchs manifested in a

32 | RESISTING ERASURE

variety of ways – including the sale of massive amounts of military hardware that turned the Gulf into the largest market for weapons in the world, economic initiatives that channelled Gulf petrodollar wealth into American financial markets, and a permanent US military presence that continues to form the ultimate guarantee of monarchical rule. A pivotal moment in the US–Gulf relationship came with the Iran–Iraq War, which lasted between 1980 and 1988, and ranks as one of the most destructive conflicts of the twentieth century (up to half a million people perished). During this war, the US supplied weapons, funding, and intelligence to both Iraq and Iran, viewing it as a way to sap the power of these two large neighbouring countries and further ensure the security of the Gulf monarchs.[17]

Despite American support for Iraqi leader Saddam Hussein during the war with Iran, US policy shifted following Hussein's invasion and occupation of Kuwait in 1990. The Gulf War of 1990–91 saw the US lead a coalition to expel Iraqi forces from Kuwait, and then impose devastating UN sanctions against Iraq, which lasted for over a decade. These sanctions, aimed at crippling the country's economy and military capabilities, killed hundreds of thousands of Iraqis. Sanctions were followed by the US/UK-led 2003 Iraq War, which overthrew Saddam Hussein and led to a significant expansion of the US military footprint in the region, including through land and naval bases across the Gulf monarchies. All of this was accompanied by a new racial discourse, the 'War on Terror', which cast Arab and Muslim communities as

FOSSIL CAPITALISM AND EMPIRE IN THE MIDDLE EAST | 33

threats and helped justify the projection of American power into the region (see Chapter 3).

Across this period, the overarching framework for US power in the region continued to rest upon two pillars: Israel, on one side, and the Gulf monarchies, on the other. There was, however, a critical shift in how these pillars related to one another. Beginning in the 1990s, and continuing through to today, the US government has sought to knit these two strategic poles together – along with other important Arab states, such as Jordan and Egypt – within a single economic and political zone aligned to US interests. For this to happen successfully, Israel needed to be integrated into the wider Middle East – by normalising its relations (economic, political, and diplomatic) with Arab states. Importantly, this meant getting rid of the formal Arab boycotts of Israel that had existed for many decades.

But the success of this kind of normalisation between Israel, Arab states, and the Gulf ultimately hinged upon there being a change in the political situation that would give a Palestinian blessing to Israel's integration into the wider region. Understanding how this came about requires a deeper look at changes to Palestinian society and politics after the 1967 occupation of the West Bank and Gaza Strip.

2

Palestinian Politics and the Oslo Accords

Tell no lies. Expose lies whenever they are told. Mask no difficulties, mistakes, failures. Claim no easy victories.

Amílcar Cabral, 'Tell No Lies,
Claim No Easy Victories . . .'

From the foundational moment of the Nakba – the ethnic cleansing of upwards of three-quarters of the Palestinian population during 1947–48 – Palestinians have endured uprooting, fragmentation, and dispersal.[1] This enduring reality has scattered Palestinians across numerous territories and political jurisdictions, illustrated in the various categories used to describe the Palestinian people: Palestinian refugees (now the largest body of refugees in the world); Palestinians who remained on their land in 1948 and later became Israeli citizens; the fragmentation of the West Bank into isolated cantons; the separation of the West Bank and Gaza Strip; and the division of Jerusalem from the West Bank.

This fragmented existence is a direct outgrowth of the logics of settler colonialism. Much like the South African Bantustan model – which itself was inspired by nineteenth-century Canadian policies towards Indigenous peoples[2] – Israeli settler colonialism has sought to weaken any sense of Palestinian collective identity, splintering the population across a patchwork of discrete and separated territories. Resistance to this process of fragmentation has been a constant theme of Palestinian politics, with a deep insistence by the Palestine Liberation Organization for most of its history that Palestinians share a common national struggle (underlined by the Right of Return of Palestinian refugees), regardless of where they may be located.

But one of the consequences of this ongoing territorial fragmentation has been the creation of distinct Palestinian social formations, each with their own specific forms of economic existence and governance, class hierarchies, and political institutions. Understanding the ways these social formations have evolved – and their connections to capitalism in both Israel and across the wider region – is fundamental to unpacking the regional trajectories of the last two decades.

A key part to this story is the Oslo Accords, an agreement signed between the PLO and the Israeli government in 1993. Oslo led to the establishment of the Palestinian Authority, a political leadership that has supplanted the PLO, and is now headquartered in the town of Ramallah, in the West Bank. The PA – led for nearly two decades by the eighty-nine-year-old Mahmoud Abbas (Abu Mazen) – is widely derided by most Palestinians. It continues to collaborate directly with the Israeli occupation, including facilitating the arrest of activists by Israeli military forces. Nonetheless, as an institution, the PA is heavily promoted (and funded) by leading Western and Arab states as the sole address for Palestinian political decision-making. As such, it is necessary to review how the PA came into being, and its deep connection to the social transformations that have taken place in the West Bank and Gaza Strip since 1967.

From 1967 to the First Intifada

With the military occupation of the West Bank and Gaza Strip in 1967, Israeli political leaders held two counterposed perspectives on what to do with the newly conquered territories.[3] Some Israeli leaders advocated incorporating these areas into Israel, viewing them as an indivisible part of the so-called Zionist homeland. Others, however, opposed this, fearing that it would mean extension of citizenship to Palestinians in the West Bank and Gaza Strip, potentially undermining the majority-Jewish character of the Israeli state. This second perspective eventually won the debate, and a military government was established that would come to control every aspect of life in the occupied territories without extending citizenship to their Palestinian inhabitants (unlike those Palestinians who remained in what became Israel after 1948). Instead, Palestinians in the West Bank and Gaza Strip carried ID cards and were subject to Israeli military law.[4] The military governor, a high-ranking officer in the Israeli military accountable only to the prime minister, would be the final arbiter regarding all decisions in the territories.

Closely related to such demographic debates was the question of land. Immediately after the 1967 occupation, Israel began to confiscate Palestinian land and build Israeli-only settlements in areas from which Palestinians had been expelled during the war (in the West Bank, for instance, about 20 per cent of the Palestinian population were driven off their lands in 1967).[5] This project was codified in the Allon Plan, named for Yigal Allon, an Israeli general and deputy prime minister from the Israeli Labour Party following 1967. Allon sought to locate Israeli settlements between major Palestinian population centres and on top of aquifers and fertile agricultural land. In the classic style of colonial conquest, this seizure of fertile land and water made Palestinians almost completely dependent on Israeli food imports. In the case of the West Bank, it also enabled Israel to expropriate large quantities of water for use inside Israel proper (by the late 1970s, this was equivalent to about one-third of Israel's water consumption).

Such destruction of agricultural life – and the overall conditions of social existence in the West Bank and Gaza Strip – meant that Palestinian markets were increasingly integrated into the much larger Israeli economy. Local industries were weakened as Israeli-produced foods and manufactured goods flooded Palestinian areas. Industrial activities that did emerge, such as textiles and leather, were usually subcontracted from Israeli companies and concentrated in very small workshops of fewer than five people.[6] Some Palestinian merchants were granted rights to distribute Israeli-produced commodities in the occupied territories, but these were typically individuals who also collaborated politically with the Israeli military. Others worked as labour subcontractors, earning commission by providing Israel with a daily supply of Palestinian workers.

Alongside such economic dependency, a complex military-bureaucratic apparatus emerged that tied a layer of Palestinians to the Israeli military occupation. Israel's aim here was to present a Palestinian face to the occupation, and various institutions were set up to achieve this goal. For instance, in 1981, Israel established the Civil Administration, which employed thousands of Palestinians as frontline police in Palestinian cities and villages in the West Bank and Gaza Strip. In the West Bank, Israel attempted to set up a network of so-called Village Leagues as an alternative to the outlawed Palestine Liberation Organization (at the time, the PLO operated mostly outside of the country, and had oriented towards a Palestinian-led struggle in the wake of the defeats suffered by Arab nationalist movements in 1967).[7] Nonetheless, despite Israel's

40 | RESISTING ERASURE

attempt to promote such institutions, they were widely rejected. Village League representatives were assassinated by activists, and most of the Palestinian population continued to regard the PLO (and the various political factions that constituted it) as their sole legitimate representative, despite its illegality.

All these developments had a profound effect on both Israeli and Palestinian capitalism. For Israel, the occupied territories significantly increased the size of Israel's domestic market, providing a captive consumer base and a source of cheap and highly exploitable labour. Commuting daily into Israel to work in sectors such as construction, agriculture, and industry, Palestinians filled the lowest rungs of the Israeli labour market and covered some of the labour shortfall caused by prolonged military service for the Jewish citizens of Israel. Through the 1970s, this labour helped underpin an economic expansion in Israel that was dubbed the 'Palestinian boom'. By the mid-1980s, Palestinians from the occupied territories made up some 7 per cent of the Israeli labour force.[8] Roughly one-third of the West Bank labour force worked in Israel in 1985,[9] with around half this number employed in the construction industry – a vital sector for the large business conglomerates that sat at the heart of the Israeli economy. The integration of Palestinian labour into the Israeli economy not only served Israel's economic needs, but further solidified Israel's control over the West Bank and Gaza Strip by making Palestinian livelihoods dependent upon access to employment in Israel.

For Palestinians, such changes meant that a generation of youth became wage earners with independent sources of income for the first time.[10] In the West Bank, which had been largely rural-based when it was ruled by Jordan between 1948 and 1967, Palestinian society became much more proletarianised and urban over the 1970s and 1980s.[11] The hierarchical and traditional structures of rural life began to erode. Such changes were reinforced by the growth of the Palestinian national movement outside the country – most notably the Palestinian resistance movements that had shaken Jordan's Hashemite monarchy through the 1970s, and then fought the Israeli occupation and its domestic collaborators in Lebanon. Palestinian political factions transmitted this politicised atmosphere to the West Bank and Gaza Strip, particularly among the generation attending university for the first time.

As part of this resurgence of the national movement, the leading Palestinian parties that made up the PLO – including Fatah, the Popular Front for the Liberation of Palestine (PFLP), the Democratic Front for the Liberation of Palestine (DFLP), and the Palestine Communist Party (PCP), extended their political networks throughout the West Bank and Gaza Strip – organising in universities, schools, and labour unions.[12] These activities helped politicise a new generation of youth and forced activists to confront important and practical questions around how to meaningfully organise on day-to-day issues in a situation of prolonged military occupation. However, organising tended to be highly

42 | RESISTING ERASURE

factionalised and driven by differing orientations towards the national struggle and key strategic political debates.[13]

These social changes were important factors underlying a popular mass revolt that first erupted in the Gaza Strip on 8 December 1987. Described as the First Intifada (literally, 'shaking off'), this uprising lasted into the early 1990s and was a historic turning point in the Palestinian struggle. Israel's initial response was characteristically violent, with the then defence minister Yitzhak Rabin calling on the military to 'break the bones' of stone-throwing youths. Israeli soldiers and civilians killed around 1,500 Palestinians, including an estimated 300 children through the years of the uprising, with thousands more suffering severe injuries. Tens of thousands of Palestinians were imprisoned without charge or trial.[14]

Alongside such military repression of the uprising, Israel also introduced a range of new bureaucratic methods aimed at controlling how Palestinians could move around the West Bank and Gaza Strip. This included the widespread deployment of curfews, zoning restrictions, and the use of permits, passes, and military checkpoints to control entry and exit from Palestinian areas. By February 1988, travel between the West Bank and Gaza Strip had become almost impossible due to Israeli restrictions. On 15 and 17 March 1988, these restrictions were officially codified in two Israeli military orders that prevented movement between the two areas. In 1989, for the first time, coloured ID cards were issued to Palestinians in the West Bank and Gaza Strip that indicated whether the bearer was a former political prisoner or considered politically active. This allowed soldiers to immediately identify and restrict the movement of activists.

In the Gaza Strip, a regulation was passed on 15 May 1989, requiring magnetic ID cards for Palestinians wanting to enter Israel for work. All these various institutional innovations laid the basis for the pass system that developed through the 1990s and 2000s, fully controlling not only passage between the West Bank and the Gaza Strip but also the ability of Palestinians to move inside these territories. This pass system mirrors bureaucratic and racialised mechanisms that have been similarly deployed by other settler-colonial states – such as the US, Canada and South Africa – to control the movement of Indigenous populations.[15]

The Oslo Accords

The First Intifada came to an end with the Oslo Accords. Officially known as the Declaration of Principles on Interim Self-Government Arrangements, this agreement was signed between the Palestine Liberation Organization (PLO) and the Israeli government under the auspices of the US in September 1993. In the celebratory pronouncements of the time, Oslo was heavily promoted as a 'peace process' – hailed as bringing 'an end to decades of confrontation and conflict', enabling the recognition of 'mutual legitimate and political

44 | RESISTING ERASURE

rights', and achieving 'peaceful coexistence and mutual dignity and security and . . . a just, lasting and comprehensive peace settlement'.

In reality, Oslo built heavily upon Israel's strategic logic since 1967, which sought to cultivate a Palestinian leadership that would administer 'self-rule' in the West Bank and Gaza Strip on behalf of Israel. Within the Oslo Accords framework, this was to take place under the leadership of members of the PLO, who returned from exile proclaiming that a Palestinian state would soon be established in the West Bank and Gaza Strip. The returning PLO cadre helped to constitute the Palestinian Authority (PA), a Palestinian government with limited powers that were elaborated in Oslo and other agreements signed during the 1990s.

Oslo divided the West Bank into Areas A, B, and C. The PA was given autonomy in Area A, at that stage constituting around 3 per cent of the West Bank and home to 20 per cent of the Palestinian population. Another 70 per cent of the Palestinian population lived in Area B, comprising 24 per cent of the West Bank, over which the PA and Israel shared joint authority. Israel fully controlled Area C, with more than 70 per cent of the territory.[16] Through this division, the Oslo Accords and subsequent agreements essentially transferred front-line responsibility for Israeli security to a Palestinian proxy, in this case the PA, while all strategic levers, particularly economic ones, remained in Israeli hands.

The means of this control had been largely set out in the preceding decades. While illegal Israeli settlements were designated a 'final status' issue under Oslo, to be negotiated over a longer period, the Israeli government launched a massive settlement expansion immediately after signing the accords, by offering large economic incentives for Israeli settlers to relocate to the West Bank and Gaza Strip. The number of settlers doubled between 1994 and the beginning of the 2000s. Focusing on strategic locations such as hill-tops and water aquifers, large settlement blocs cut across the West Bank, preventing the natural growth of Palestinian population centres. The settlements were to be connected by another Oslo-era innovation, the so-called bypass roads, restricted-access highways that connect settlement blocs with one another and with Israeli cities.

The net effect of these measures meant that the 90 per cent of the Palestinian population living in Areas A and B in the West Bank were confined to a patchwork of isolated enclaves, with three main clusters in the northern, central, and southern sections of the territory, separated from one another by settlement blocs. Travel between these areas could be shut down at any time by the Israeli military using checkpoints and military personnel. All entry to and from Areas A and B, as well as the determination of residency rights in these areas, were under Israeli authority.

Likewise, access to Jerusalem was progressively cut off from surrounding Palestinian areas. This was significant not simply for religious reasons, but because Jerusalem had long served as a primary market, employment centre, and node of financial and commercial

46 | RESISTING ERASURE

activity for the West Bank.[17] To achieve this separation, Israel built a ring of Israeli-only settlements and roads surrounding Jerusalem. It also deployed a familiar combination of physical and bureaucratic means, including the construction of permanent checkpoints, the use of special permits, and, later, a sprawling concrete wall dubbed the Apartheid Wall that restricted Palestinian access to the city.

This spatial fragmentation was further reinforced through infrastructure development, which served to solidify Israeli control. The electricity sector remained almost entirely dependent on the Israeli Electric Corporation, with Palestinian providers forced to act primarily as payment collectors rather than independent utilities, and new electricity infrastructure projects requiring Israeli approval.[18] Similarly, telecommunications, including internet connectivity, was constrained by Israeli control over electromagnetic space and physical networks: Palestinian internet traffic was routed through Israeli servers, and the installation of telecommunications infrastructure required permits that were often delayed or denied.[19]

This system of managed dependence extended to all resources: Israel controlled the vast majority of aquifers, all underground resources, and all air space. Whereas Israel used close to 500 million cubic meters of water annually by the late 1990s, Palestinians in the West Bank used only 105 million.[20] A similar structure existed in the Gaza Strip, with the PA given 'autonomy' and Israel retaining control over settlements and military bases. Permits were even required for Gazan fisherfolk to use the sea. Likewise, the entry and exit of goods and people from the Gaza Strip came under Israeli control. Movement between Gaza and the West Bank was made virtually impossible, with Israel rendering the two areas separate entities. Rather than creating the foundations for an independent Palestinian state, these Oslo-era economic and infrastructural arrangements created a system where Palestinian development remained fundamentally tied to and constrained by Israeli oversight and approval mechanisms.

Underpinning these overt forms of Israeli control, the means of repression in the West Bank and Gaza Strip were subcontracted to the newly formed Palestinian Authority. The PA security forces, funded and openly trained by Western military and intelligence agencies, received the largest component of the Palestinian budget. Money went to the training of new Palestinian police and intelligence forces as well as the construction of new prisons. Since the signing of Oslo through to the current moment, these Palestinian security forces remain in constant communication with the Israeli military, and at times of heightened political upheaval in the West Bank (for instance, since October 2023) have worked to facilitate the entry of Israeli soldiers into Palestinian towns and villages for the purposes of arresting or assassinating activists.

A Disposable Reserve Army of Labour

As movement restrictions took stronger hold under Oslo, the characteristics of Palestinian labour were transformed. Increasingly, Israel sought to bring in foreign migrant workers as a replacement for Palestinians from the West Bank and Gaza Strip. One reason for this shift was a reorganisation of the Israeli economy away from construction and agriculture towards high-tech industries and exports of finance capital in the 1990s. Strikes and labour organising among Palestinian workers during the years of the First Intifada had also created difficulties for Israeli employers. While foreign workers from places like Thailand, the Philippines, or Romania were more costly than Palestinians, they were highly exploitable because of their precarious visa status and thus easier to control.

In turn, Palestinian labour from the West Bank and Gaza Strip became a larger reserve supply of workers that could be turned on and off, depending on the economic and political situation and the needs of the Israeli economy. Between 1992 and 1996, Palestinian employment in Israel (from the West Bank and Gaza Strip) declined from 116,000 workers (33 per cent of the Palestinian labour force) to 28,100 (6 per cent of the Palestinian labour force). Earnings from work in Israel collapsed from 25 per cent of Palestinian GNP in 1992 to 6 per cent in 1996.[21] Between 1997 and 1999, an upturn in the Israeli economy saw the numbers of Palestinian workers increase to approximately pre-1993 levels, but the proportion of the Palestinian labour force working in Israel had almost halved compared with a decade earlier. These patterns confirm that Palestinian labour from the West Bank and Gaza Strip had increasingly become a captive and highly flexible reserve army for Israeli capitalism.[22]

At the same time, many Palestinians became dependent on either PA public sector employment or meagre transfer payments made by the PA to families of political prisoners, those killed by the Israeli military, or the poor. By 2000, public sector employment made up nearly one-quarter of total employment in the West Bank and Gaza Strip, a level that had almost doubled since the mid-1990s. More than half the PA's expenditure went to salaries of these public sector workers. The other major source of employment was the private sector, particularly in the area of services. This was overwhelmingly dominated by very small, family-owned businesses due to decades of Israeli de-development policies (over 90 per cent of Palestinian private sector businesses employ fewer than ten people).

A Captive Economy

The pronounced economic dependency of Palestinians in the West Bank and Gaza Strip on the PA developed in parallel with the continuing subordination of the Palestinian economy to Israel. This subordination was formalised in the 1994 Paris Protocol, an economic agreement signed between the PA and Israel as part of the Oslo process, which established a customs union between Israel and the Palestinian territories.[23] Under this arrangement, the PA was forced to adopt Israeli import policies and tariff rates, effectively binding the Palestinian economy to Israeli trade policy. Palestinian importers had to use Israeli ports and airports, paying customs duties to Israeli authorities, with those revenues then meant to be transferred to the PA. This created a system where even basic economic activities required Israeli mediation and approval, making it impossible to develop independent trade relationships or protect nascent Palestinian industries.

Israel also controlled the entry and exit of all goods and people into the West Bank and Gaza Strip. This further exacerbated the dependency of the Palestinian population on goods manufactured and imported from Israel. By 2005, the Palestinian Central Bureau of Statistics estimated that 74 per cent of all imports to the West Bank and Gaza Strip originated in Israel, while 88 per cent of exports were destined for Israel. As part of the Paris Protocol, Palestinians were also tied to using the Israeli shekel as their currency. This left the monetary system beholden to Israeli monetary policy, and regular bouts of severe inflation served to benefit Israeli companies (because prices were high) and drained wealth from the occupied territories to Israel.[24]

Much of the PA's income came from indirect taxes collected by the Israeli government on goods imported from abroad and destined for the occupied territories. This tax was collected by the Israeli government and

PALESTINIAN POLITICS AND THE OSLO ACCORDS | 51

then transferred to the PA each month, according to a process outlined in the Paris Protocol. Whenever the Israeli government chose for political reasons to withhold payment of this money (as it has repeatedly done), the PA faced a major fiscal crisis. Indeed, shortly before Israel's war on Gaza, taxes collected by Israel made up around half of the PA's income.[25] The other primary source of the PA's income comes from aid and foreign disbursements by the United States, Europe, and Arab governments. Such disbursements have made Palestinians among the most 'aid-dependent' peoples in the world.[26] And with such a large proportion of the population working for the PA (in sectors such as education, health, or security), the reliance on this external funding has also shaped the political mood.

Given these structural features of the Palestinian economy, a Palestinian capitalist class also emerged with a very distinctive character. Following the population expulsions of 1948 and 1967, the wealthiest components of Palestinian society relocated to *outside* of Palestine. Initially, this diaspora bourgeoisie was mostly displaced to Lebanon and Jordan, but with the dramatic expansion of Gulf economies in the 1970s, prominent Palestinian businesspeople made their homes in Saudi Arabia and the other Gulf monarchies. Here, they were integrated into the development of capitalism in the Gulf, establishing large business conglomerates spanning construction, finance, retail and other sectors. In numerous cases, these Palestinian businesspeople were also granted Gulf citizenship – a privilege that is impossible for the vast majority of migrant workers in the Gulf.

Following the Oslo Accords, some parts of this diaspora bourgeoisie 'returned' to Palestine, where they formed a key social base of the PA. Other principal components of Palestinian capital came from established elites, particularly large pre-1967 landowners in the West Bank, as well as those who had managed to accumulate power as interlocutors with the Israeli occupation after 1967. These social layers drew wealth from their advantageous connection to the PA, including receiving agency rights for the import and distribution of goods such as petrol, steel, cement, and tobacco. As a class, they have been integral to pushing forward neoliberal economic policies developed by the World Bank and other international financial institutions.[27] Such policies included cuts to PA public spending and privatisation, with continued donor funding conditional on their implementation. Debt and inequality levels increased massively in the West Bank and Gaza Strip (alongside a large divergence in social and economic conditions between the two territories). The only sector of the Palestinian budget untouched by austerity was spending on security and internal repression.

Although representing a very small layer of Palestinian society, the wealth of this new Palestinian capitalist class grew substantially. Concentrated largely in the West Bank, they came to dominate the ownership of major economic sectors such as banking and real estate.[28] The expansion of their business networks took place through direct investments, as well as the formation of large holding companies that linked this class to PA institutions. Importantly, however, the leading segments of Palestinian capital continued to see their main zone of capital accumulation *outside* of Palestine – notably in the Gulf states.[29]

In sum, the territorial outcome of the Oslo process was the severance of the West Bank and Gaza Strip from one another, and the fragmentation of the West Bank into isolated cantons separated by Israeli settlement blocs. The PA held direct authority over most Palestinians living in these areas. But the Palestinian economy was fully subordinated to Israeli capitalism through military-backed restrictions on movement, Israeli control over borders, and the almost complete fiscal reliance of the PA on external capital flows. Palestinian labour was concentrated in either low-paid work in Israel (which could be shut down at any point through the restriction on movements and permits) or in the PA public sector (which was dependent on foreign funding). A tiny layer of wealthy Palestinian capital was tightly connected to the PA and political decision-making, but with most of their main business activities located outside the occupied territories.

The Regional Dimension

Beyond these implications for processes of Palestinian class and state formation, Oslo was a driving force in facilitating the regional trajectories highlighted in the previous chapter: the US-led integration of Israel into the wider Middle East through the normalisation of relations with Arab states (especially the Gulf). From Israel's perspective, this was not simply about enabling Israeli trade with, and investments in, Arab states. Following a severe recession in the mid-1980s, Israel's economy had shifted away from sectors such as construction and agriculture, towards a much greater emphasis on high-tech, finance, and military exports. Many leading international companies, however, were reluctant to do business with Israeli firms (or inside Israel itself) because of the secondary boycotts imposed by Arab governments.[30] Dropping these boycotts was essential to attracting big Western firms into Israel, and also to enabling access by Israeli firms to foreign markets in the US and elsewhere. Economic normalisation, in other words, was just as much about ensuring Israeli capitalism's place in the global economy as it was about Israel accessing markets in the Middle East.

The establishment of the PA facilitated this regional transformation, as it provided a Palestinian 'green light' to normalisation. Through the 1990s, Oslo meant that Israel could portray its intentions as those of a partner rather than an enemy of Palestinian sovereignty. Backed by the PA's reliance on foreign funding, the US and European governments promoted a range of schemes that sought to link Israel with Arab states. A major part of this was the deepening of neoliberal economic reforms in the Middle East through the 1990s and early

2000s – an opening up to foreign investment and trade flows, which also aimed at creating close economic ties between Israel and Arab economies.

These trajectories initially came together in a series of intergovernmental meetings held annually between 1994 and 1998, known as the MENA Economic Summits. According to the Jordanian Foreign Ministry, the summits 'intended to create economic interdependencies between Arab states and Israel, promote personal contacts between the two sides and foster trade, investment and development'.[31] Along these lines, the first MENA summit was held in Casablanca, Morocco, and agreed to take measures to lift the regional economic boycott of Israel and also to establish a Middle East Chamber of Commerce – with the then US secretary of state, Warren Christopher, enthusing that 'the Middle East is open for business . . . the conference could be the beginning of a beautiful friendship.'[32] The clear neoliberal orientation of these meetings was expressed in the 1996 gathering, convened in Cairo, Egypt, which noted: 'The region's economic, commercial and trade potential . . . is being greatly enhanced by important economic reform programs currently being undertaken by many states in the region. These reforms, which include privatisation, structural reform, and removing trade barriers, have provided for a more business-friendly economic climate throughout the region.'[33]

Importantly, however, this twinning of liberalisation and normalisation was explicitly accompanied by a deepening of US economic and political influence in the region. One indication of this was the Qualifying Industrial Zones programme (QIZs), which aimed to tie Israeli and Arab markets to one another through the mediation of the US economy. These low-wage manufacturing zones were first established in Jordan and Egypt in the late 1990s. Goods produced in the QIZs (mostly textiles and garments) were given duty-free access to the US. To gain this access, however, they had to be jointly produced with Israeli investors. Through this crucial requirement, the QIZs played an early and decisive role in bringing together Israeli, Jordanian, and Egyptian capital in joint ownership structures under US influence – normalising economic relations between two of the Arab states that neighbour Israel. By 2007, the US government was reporting that more than 70 per cent of Jordan's exports to the US came from QIZs; for Egypt, 30 per cent of exports to the US were produced in QIZs in 2008.[34]

Alongside the QIZ programme, the US also proposed the Middle East Free Trade Area (MEFTA) initiative in 2003, which aimed to establish a free trade zone spanning the entire region by 2013. The US strategy was to negotiate individually with 'friendly' countries using a graduated six-step process that would eventually lead to a full-fledged free trade agreement (FTA) between the US and the country in question. These FTAs were designed so that countries could connect with other countries' bilateral FTAs, thereby establishing sub-regional-level agreements across the Middle East. These sub-regional agreements could be linked over time,

PALESTINIAN POLITICS AND THE OSLO ACCORDS | 57

until they covered the entire region. Importantly, these FTAs would also be used to encourage Israel's integration into Arab markets, with each agreement containing a clause committing the signatory to normalisation with Israel and forbidding any boycott of trade relations. While the US failed to meet its 2013 goal for establishing MEFTA, the policy successfully drove an expansion of US economic influence in the region, underpinned by normalisation between Israel and key Arab states. Pointedly, today the US has fourteen FTAs with countries across the world: five of these are with states in the Middle East (Israel, Bahrain, Morocco, Jordan, and Oman).

The Afterlives of Oslo

As with every attempt to liquidate the Palestinian struggle, the Oslo process came apart following a new uprising that erupted across the West Bank and Gaza Strip in September 2000. In quelling this 'Second Intifada', Israel deployed similar strategies to the earlier uprising: curfews and collective punishment, killings, and destruction of infrastructure. A key element of this repression was the extensive system of political imprisonment, which saw tens of thousands of Palestinians detained, tortured, and imprisoned under Israeli military law, some without charge or trial.[35] At the same time, a range of control mechanisms that had developed under Oslo were particularly effective tools of Israeli repression. This included the shutting down of movement between

Palestinian areas, restrictions on trade, and the withholding of payments to the PA. This was also the moment in which Israel began construction of its so-called Apartheid Wall – a sprawling network of concrete barriers and electric fences that now surrounds major Palestinian areas in the West Bank.

The Second Intifada and its aftermath are often described as marking the end of Oslo and any hopes of enduring 'peace'. The problem with this way of thinking about Oslo is that it misunderstands both the content of the negotiation process and its fundamental continuum with the current moment. From the perspective of the US, EU, and Israel, Oslo was never about ending the occupation of the West Bank and Gaza Strip or addressing the substantive issues of Palestinian dispossession. It was rather a fig leaf for deepening Israeli control and the further fragmentation of the Palestinian people.

One side to this was the pernicious political effect of Oslo. By reducing the Palestinian struggle to the process of bartering over slivers of land in the West Bank and Gaza Strip, it ideologically disarmed the Palestinian political movement. Palestinian citizens of Israel and Palestinian refugees living outside Palestine (the majority of the Palestinian people) were progressively marginalised from national politics.[36] Oslo also pushed aside the key demand of the Palestinian struggle – the right of Palestinian refugees to return to their homes and lands, normalising an illusory pragmatism rather than tackling the foundational roots of Palestinian exile. Internationally,

Oslo undermined the widespread solidarity and sympathy with the Palestinian struggle built during the years of the First Intifada, replacing an orientation toward grassroots collective mobilisation with a faith in negotiations steered by Western governments.

The Oslo process had a particularly sharp impact on the Gaza Strip. Initially, the economic vision promoted under Oslo framed Gaza as a potential 'Singapore on the Sea'. This vision was predicated on the idea that Gaza's coastal location and young population could drive rapid economic growth, trade, and tourism, turning it into a regional hub. Reflecting a deeply neoliberal framework, this development strategy prioritised market-driven growth and external investment over genuine justice. Its net effect was simply to exacerbate inequalities, deepening Gaza's dependence on foreign aid and Israeli control.

In 2005, Israel unilaterally evacuated all Israeli settlers and dismantled military infrastructure in the Gaza Strip. This so-called disengagement was portrayed as an 'end' to Israeli presence in the territory. In reality, it was a calculated strategic move, enabling Israel to remove the costs of protecting settlements and settlers in Gaza, while tightening its domination through the control of borders, airspace, and coastal waters. Far from ending Israeli control, the disengagement increased Gaza's dependence on Israel for essentials like electricity, fuel, and food. At the same time, the Strip became a testing ground for advanced strategies of domination.[37] The closure regime tightened and buffer zones along the borders were militarised, restricting Palestinian movement and access to farmland. Aerial surveillance and airstrikes replaced ground patrols, enabling Israel to exercise dominance while minimising risks to its forces. Crucially, the absence of settlers allowed Israel to unleash more frequent and devastating military campaigns, without endangering any of its own citizens.

The full implications of this system of control were made clear in 2007, after the West Bank and Gaza Strip were formally divided into two separately administered territories ruled by the PA and Hamas respectively.[38] Since that time, Israel has imposed a brutal siege on Gaza and launched six major wars – in 2008, 2012, 2014, 2018, 2021, and now 2023 – that have devastated Gaza's infrastructure and economy.[39] The blockade of the Strip decimated key sectors like agriculture and fishing, driving unemployment rates to staggering levels. (In 2022, the unemployment rate in the Gaza Strip was 47 per cent, one of the highest in the world, with youth unemployment reaching 64 per cent.[40])

The destruction of Gaza's infrastructure by repeated bombardment worsened this economic situation, leading to chronic shortages of vital resources like water and electricity. As a result, 80 per cent of Gaza's population became dependent on international aid for survival. Hamas attempted to develop its own economic and political networks, including turning to foreign aid from countries like Qatar. It also attempted to evade the blockade by bringing in goods through underground tunnels running into Egypt.[41] Nonetheless, Gaza's almost complete isolation kept the economy in a state of controlled collapse, callously described by Israeli officials as putting the population of the territory 'on a diet'.[42]

The situation facing the people of Gaza prior to October 2023 confirms that Palestinian dispossession has never been solely a consequence of Israeli military force: it has always simultaneously depended upon an all-encompassing system of bureaucratic control, movement restrictions, and economic blockade. These mechanisms were made a reality through the US-backed negotiations of the 1990s, a process ultimately aimed at deepening Israel's integration into the wider region. For all these reasons we must remember the Oslo process in clear continuity with what exists today: a direct thread connects the 1990s to the 2023–24 Israeli genocide in Gaza.

3

Racialising Palestine

In reality, a colonial country is a racist country.
Frantz Fanon, 'Racism and Culture'

The oppression of Palestinians is deeply rooted in the structures of fossil capitalism and settler colonialism. However, these structures cannot be understood without recognising how they have always been reinforced, justified, and sustained through racism. Anti-Palestinian racism serves as an ideological tool to legitimise Israel's settler-colonial expansion; it has also shaped the way Palestinians are governed, dispossessed, and repressed.

The forms of this racism stem directly from the character of Israeli settler-colonial capitalism. There is a racialised social division based on the superiority of the settler population, which is embedded in the very constitutional structure of Israel. This was most recently on display with the enactment of the 2018 'Basic Law: Israel as the Nation-State of the Jewish People', (re)confirming the nature of Israel as a Jewish state in which the 'realization of the right to exercise national self-determination . . . is unique to the Jewish people'. In defining the state along these lines, such laws signify the structural exclusion of Palestinian citizens of Israel – a population that now makes up around 20 per cent of the state's total citizens. The exclusion of Palestinians is not just a byproduct of Israeli state policy – it is foundational to its existence.

Throughout the West Bank and Gaza Strip, racial structures of settler colonialism have taken different forms based on military occupation, economic blockade, and a system of bureaucratic control governing every aspect of Palestinian life. In the West Bank, a key element to this is the unending expansion of the settlement project itself: ensuring Israeli settlers have full political and economic rights while Palestinians are subjected to military rule, land seizures, and violent displacement.

Anti-Palestinian racism is not something incidental to these structures of settler colonialism and it is not something that can be reduced to prejudice, discrimination, or unequal access to rights. Palestinians become legitimate targets of violence – both at the hands of the Israeli military and of Israeli citizens – through their racialisation. Anti-Palestinian racism makes it possible to justify policies of ethnic cleansing, torture, starvation, and blockade. In short, Israeli settler-colonial capitalism functions *through* its racialisation of Palestinians; and it is this process of racialisation that produces anti-Palestinian racism.[1]

Importantly, anti-Palestinian racism does not operate in a singular or static way; it functions across multiple interconnected scales. Beyond Israel itself, it helps uphold and reproduce the structures of imperial power globally. Western governments provide military aid, economic support, and diplomatic cover for Israeli actions, while also suppressing pro-Palestinian voices through censorship, criminalisation, and legislation targeting activist movements. This support is justified through broader Islamophobic and anti-Arab narratives that reinforce racialised fears of Muslim and Arab populations.

For this reason, the racial logics that enable Israel's settler colonialism are deeply intertwined with state violence more broadly. The same legal and security apparatuses used to police Palestinian activism – anti-terror laws, surveillance, restrictions on protest – are also deployed against other racialised communities worldwide, reinforcing racial hierarchies that position them as threats to be monitored and controlled. Recognising these interconnected layers is part of building an anti-racist politics of Palestine solidarity – one that does not isolate Palestine as an exception, but situates it within the bigger structures of an always-racialised global capitalism.

The racial hierarchies that underpin Israel's settler-colonial project did not emerge in isolation; they are part of a longer history of colonial expansion and imperial domination. Palestine's position within the Ottoman Empire, and later under British colonial rule,

66 | RESISTING ERASURE

shaped the conditions for Zionist settlement and the racial frameworks that continue to structure Palestinian exclusion. To grasp how racism operates in the present, we must examine how it was embedded in the processes of colonial partition, forced displacement, and economic control that culminated in the Nakba and continue – in new forms – to define Palestinian life today.

Racism, Colonialism, and the Nakba

In recent history, Palestine was a region of the Ottoman Empire. The Ottoman Empire itself had occupied an ambiguous place in the emergent international capitalist order through the eighteenth and nineteenth centuries. During this time, the Ottoman Empire represented a relatively powerful rival – and obstacle – to European colonial ambitions in the lands that would later become known as the 'Middle East'. As a Muslim polity, the Ottoman Empire was both fetishised and feared in European narratives: romanticised as an exotic land of cultural mystique while simultaneously cast as a backward, menacing force in need of subjugation or reform. This contradictory framing reflected broader colonial anxieties about non-European sovereignty and resistance to imperial expansion.

At the time, the international legal regime governing the rights and protection of societies was a directly racist one, based around a European 'standard of civilisation'. This standard – very literally drawing together racism and capitalism – meant that only societies which had adopted European social practices, that is to say, capitalist ones, had legal rights and protections.[2]

This standard was not simply designed to *exclude* non-European states but also served as an impetus to social transformation: if non-European states sufficiently reformed their economies and protected European investments, they could be recognised by the European powers and included in 'Civilisation'. For this reason, the Ottoman Empire concluded a number of highly unequal treaties in which Europeans resident in the Empire would be governed by the domestic laws of their own countries.[3]

So when the Ottoman Empire entered the First World War – on the side of Germany – it did so on an already racialised and largely subordinated basis. This racialised subordination was central to justifying British (and French) attitudes towards the region, most particularly the belief that they had the right to partition the Ottoman Empire and place it under European rule. In the case of Palestine, this was expressed through Britain's issuance of the Balfour Declaration in 1917, in which the British state undertook to establish a 'national home for the Jewish people' in Palestine.[4]

This racism was matched by that of the Zionist movement itself, which was centred in Europe and appealed to a series of racist characterisations rooted in European colonialism. Ideas such as 'a land without a people, a people without a land' and 'making the desert bloom' played on the sense that – because of their lack of 'industriousness' and 'productivity' – the 'uncivilised' Arabs in Palestine were undeserving of legal and political rights. As such, they were entitled to be dispossessed of their lands and 'civilised' by the advanced Europeans.[5]

These were not simply *ideas*. At the end of the First World War, they were directly codified in the League of Nations Mandate System. The Mandate System was designed to deal with the colonies of the defeated powers which were – in the racist words of the League Covenant – 'not yet able to stand by themselves under the strenuous conditions of the modern world'. Reproducing, once again, the direct racism of colonialism, the Mandate System placed these territories under the 'tutelage' of 'advanced nations'.[6]

This language of racist humanitarianism, of helping the 'backwards', enabled the victorious powers to pursue their projects of colonisation in the region. This was particularly important for Britain during the 1910s and 1920s. At that time, the British Empire was centred on India and wider South Asia, and what happened in the former lands of the neighbouring Ottoman Empire was key to maintaining overall colonial rule. One major focus of this was British and French control of the Suez Canal, a shipping route that directly connected the 'East' with European markets. Another critical factor was Britain's goal of securing oil supplies in the Middle East. In 1911, the British government had taken the decision to power its naval fleet with oil rather than coal, and this meant – as Winston Churchill, then head of the

British Admiralty, put it – that Britain needed to 'to draw [its] oil supply, so far as possible, from sources under British control or British influence'. The principal target here was Iran, where the British-run Anglo-Persian Oil Company controlled all oil extraction and refining (a company we today know as BP).[7]

In this context, Britain – considered the 'tutor' of Palestine under the Mandate System – sought to strengthen its dominance in the region by encouraging the migration of European Jewish settlers to Palestine. In so doing, the British state relied on a plethora of racist colonial arguments that underpinned the Mandate System and consciously disregarded the positions of the existing inhabitants of Palestine.[8] This process, of course, culminated in 1947–48 in the Nakba, as the newly settled Jewish population expelled hundreds of thousands of Palestinians from their lands.

Here we can see the multiple levels on which race and racism functioned to secure and advance the interests of British capitalism in the region. The British state's support for a Jewish homeland in Palestine was premised on the possibility of projecting British power, and capital, in the Middle East. In this respect, the creation of the state of Israel was understood as a way of creating a loyal, 'civilised' entity that would buttress Britain's position against any Arab nationalist movements or attempts by the peoples of the region to chart an independent course after the fragmentation of the Ottoman Empire.[9]

This was undergirded by an institutionalised racism in the form of the Mandate System and justified through a racist language of civilisation. Alongside this, the newly arrived settler population appealed to ideas about the wastefulness and non-productive nature of non-Europeans to justify their dispossession of the Palestinian population and the 'transformation' of their land. Racist stereotypes were thus deployed by the settlers, and the nascent Israeli state, and used to excuse the violence unleashed against resistance in the region.[10]

Founded on the expulsion of the population of Palestine from their land, ideas of racial superiority were embedded into Israeli settler colonialism from the very beginning. Yet these arguments do not simply remain in the past. The descendants of the expelled Palestinians – now the largest body of refugees in the world – continue to demand liberation and their right to return. The territory occupied by the Israeli state itself contains many non-Jewish Palestinian citizens, and borders both the West Bank and Gaza Strip, where millions more Palestinian non-citizens live. These multiple pressures mean that the settler-colonial project of Israel – to create an ethno-nation in historic Palestine – *cannot dispense* with an intrinsic and fundamental racism towards Palestinians.

Racial Logics of Settler-Colonial Capitalism: 'Security' and 'Terrorism'

Settler colonialism is often reduced to the logic of extermination – the idea that native populations must be eradicated to secure land for settlers. But as history shows, the reality is far more complex. Like all forms of colonialism, the imperatives of capital accumulation and labour exploitation are essential to how settler colonialism unfolds. A historical survey of settler-colonial experiences worldwide reveals the diversity of these forms: outright attempts at extermination; the creation of 'Bantustan' enclaves where indigenous populations are confined under a veneer of self-rule; the direct exploitation of native labour in sectors like mining and agriculture; or various combinations of these methods. The form settlement takes is not simply a question of ideology but of how the control of land, labour, and capital is exercised in any given historical moment. Many contingencies are at play here – not least, the ability of indigenous populations to resist colonisation.[11]

As we have seen, the Palestinian experience under Israeli settler colonialism has also taken multiple forms, evolving over time and shaped by the specific territorial enclaves and the ways they have been absorbed into Israeli capitalism. The mechanisms of domination – whether through expulsion and violence, direct military occupation, or economic subjugation – have never been static. These mechanisms have also been bound up with the emergence of different social forces within Palestinian society, which has been a crucial lever in how Israeli settler colonialism has operated over the past eight decades.

A common element to all these processes is the necessity of *managing* the Palestinian population, and here the racialisation of Palestinians is paramount. In the

72 | RESISTING ERASURE

present day, this racialisation has crystallised around a language of *terrorism* and the need for *security*.

Part and parcel of the Israeli state's racist projection of itself as a bastion of European civilisation has always been that it is surrounded by hostile – and uncivilised – peoples. The Palestinian people, of course, lack the organised state capacity to resist Israeli occupation, oppression, and expulsion. Their resistance therefore has always been rooted in non-state action – including armed violence but also embracing strikes, protests, and demonstrations, and seeking international solidarity through initiatives like the boycott, divestment and sanctions movement, as well as diplomatic and legal avenues.

The crucial move of the Israeli state is to isolate the use of armed force and label it as 'terrorism'. This threat of terrorism, nebulous but ever-present, is then used to characterise all Palestinian political activities and all Palestinians – especially Palestinian men – as potential terrorists.[12] In doing so, the Israeli state relies upon the pervasive (and often unconscious) racialised belief that non-Europeans are inherently threatening, violent, irrational, and untrustworthy.

Alongside serving as a powerful rhetorical justification, this racialised language of security has enabled the construction of a vast architecture of surveillance and control over Palestinians. In the West Bank, for instance, Palestinians may only travel along specific roads, are only able to enter the territory of the Israeli state (and thus move between the fragmented Palestinian territories) on a highly restrictive basis, and are governed by

Israeli military law (whereas Israeli citizens living in the same area are subject to Israeli civil law). All of this is justified by a claim to 'security'.

The sum total of these actions has led lawyers, activists, human rights organisations and others to characterise Israel as practising *apartheid*, that is to say, governance by means of systematic racial domination.[13] The Israeli state has, of course, insisted that its concerns are about security and nothing more. In this way, the language of security and terrorism has offered the Israeli state a flexible mechanism to enact the racialised management of Palestinians, while simultaneously denying its own structurally racist foundations.

Since Israel's establishment in 1948, the language of security and terrorism has also been key to justifying military violence and the selective assassination of Palestinian leaders and political figures.[14] In particular, the period of the Second Intifada (2000–04) saw Israel's assassination policy concretised through the development of an expansive legal framework around the tactic of 'targeted killing'. In essence, the Israeli state made the argument that the threat of 'terrorist' violence from Palestinians would activate Israel's right to self-defence and thus authorise – under international law – the use of military force. Such military force could then be 'targeted' at various elements of the Palestinian political leadership.[15]

The idea of 'targeted killing' was embedded in a wider racial narrative about the *continual* threat posed by Palestinians. This supposed permanency of the Palestinian threat extends the justification for Israeli violence in both time and space. For instance, the Israeli state claims the right to strike at Palestinians and their supporters *pre-emptively* – before any attack has occurred – and *anywhere*. To take a recent example, in July 2024 the Israeli state killed Ismail Haniyeh in Tehran, Iran, acknowledging responsibility five months later. Similarly, Israel Katz, the Israeli defence minister, warned the Houthis in Yemen: 'Anyone who raises a hand against Israel will have his hand cut off, and the long arm of the IDF will strike him and hold him accountable.'[16]

In positing the Palestinian people in their entirety as a permanent threat to security, as terrorists one and all, the Israeli state thus justifies military action in 'self-defence' anytime and anywhere. The racialisation of Palestinians enables the unbounded deployment of Israeli military force.

Racial Solidarities

This kind of racialised violence has also become a direct source of profit for the Israeli state and private companies. The Israeli arms industry was the ninth-largest in the world in 2023, and the war in Gaza has helped it grow immensely. Indeed, the global arms trade monitoring group, the Stockholm International Peace Research Institute (SIPRI), reported that the top three Israeli military firms earned $13.6 billion in revenue in 2023, the highest figure ever recorded. Beyond this, the mass surveillance of Palestinians has been an active spur to the development of Israeli security technologies that are exported across the world. In short, anti-Palestinian racism is big business for Israel.[17]

It is not, however, just military and surveillance technology that is exported by the Israeli state. The language of 'targeted killing', the use of expanded military force against 'terrorists', and the assumption that every racialised person is a potential terrorist, have also become global in form. This has been the case since the launch of the 'War on Terror' in 2002, when the US deployed the same reasoning in Afghanistan, Iraq, Yemen, Syria, Somalia and more. Such arguments have also underpinned the expansion of the US drone programme – carried out under the Bush, Obama, Trump, and Biden administrations – and the constant surveillance and deployment of military force against racialised populations.[18] And while the US is the biggest exponent of this violence, similar arguments have been used by almost every imperialist power over the last twenty-five years.

The point here goes beyond the role of the Israeli state as a laboratory or crucible for these kinds of racialised justifications for imperial violence. They also grant the Israeli state a crucial role in the projection of US power in the region. The Israeli state's own security discourse dovetails almost completely with that of the US. Israel's enemies in the region are those of the US, with Israel standing as a beacon of stability. Israel's role of securing American power in the region is expressed

RESISTING ERASURE

as a kind of 'racial solidarity' that pits civilisation against barbarism. Unmoored from wider diplomatic and political responsibilities that might limit the US in the region, this enables Israel to act on behalf of the US – through direct military force as well as in a myriad other ways.

Civilised Aspirations

At the same time, it would be a mistake to imagine that these kinds of racialising projects are purely negative and coercive ones that are imposed from above. They have also been used to provide standards which peripheral states can aspire to, so that they might become 'civilised'. As such, racism has been used to divide the targets of exploitation into 'good' and 'bad' peoples. This is also true *within* countries: local ruling classes are invited to reach the 'civilised' standard, and, in the name of security, purge the 'bad' elements within their own borders.[19]

Such 'civilised aspirations' have been a key element of the War on Terror. One legal argument which the US has consistently adduced in this respect is that certain states are 'unwilling or unable' to combat terrorism (and guarantee security).[20] Accordingly, the US argues that with *these states* the US can directly exercise its right to self-defence on their territories – even if they have no connection to the various political movements supposedly operating within their borders. The task for the managers of such states – Yemen stands out in this regard – is to prove that they are 'willing and able' to be brought into the fold. As Ntina Tzouvala puts it: 'Rather than simply stigmatizing or "Othering" postcolonial states, the [War on Terror] doctrine offers them a way to protect themselves from the violent consequences of being designated as "unwilling or unable" by signing up to the political economy, politics, and aesthetics of the war on terror.'[21]

In this way, the US has used the racist language of the War on Terror to compel and manage a whole host of states in the Middle East, finding particular success in Egypt and Jordan – the frontline states for the normalisation projects discussed in earlier chapters. At the same time, the ruling classes of these states have enthusiastically adopted such arguments, as a mechanism to receive support and aid from the US *and* as a pretext to crack down on their own domestic political opposition.

The Israeli state itself represents a crucial part of this picture. Insofar as Israel is posited as a bulwark of civilisation and security in the region, acceptance of its legitimacy and existence has become a prerequisite for demonstrating a country's willingness and ability to become 'civilised'. Again, we see here the ways in which particular racialised binaries – the 'terrorist' versus those deserving of 'security' – work to affirm a broader project of regional transformation. This is why *all* the states to have formally embraced US-led normalisation with Israel – Jordan, Egypt, the UAE, Morocco, Bahrain – simultaneously deploy the language of 'security' and 'anti-terrorism' to manage their own populations.[22]

Importantly, we should note that this language is not simply addressed to states outside of Palestine: it also operates within Palestine itself. Both the US and Israel have mobilised the racialised language of security to divide Palestinian society and buttress the class configurations that emerged in the wake of the Oslo process. Insofar as all Palestinian political mobilisation is understood as potential terrorist or terrorist-supporting activity, the PA can only prove its civilised nature by acting against such activities and collaborating with both the Israeli state and the US. In this respect, the PA is incentivised to enforce these racialised notions of security, while at the same time solidifying its own power.

Ultimately, the racialised notions of security developed and deployed by the Israeli state find their mirror image in US imperial endeavours. On the one hand, these racialised discourses are 'negative', legitimising and structuring imperial violence in the region. On the other, they serve as a positive mode of binding the region's ruling classes to the US-led project of regional transformation. In both these modes the Israeli state is accorded a leading position, through the language of racial solidarity, in which Israel serves as an outpost of reliable imperial power in the region.

Security at Home

Thus far, we have seen how racial logics have animated and structured the actions of powerful actors – of states, of ruling classes, of governments and institutions. Here, the role of racism has been to justify the deployment of deadly violence and drive forward social transformation. It has created a scaffolding through which states and ruling classes can prove they are 'willing and able' to suppress their enemies in the name of 'security'.

Such racialised logics have also been part of managing popular opposition to the Israeli state at a global level. The most obvious set of mechanisms here are those embedded in the War on Terror's domestic framework. Besides authorising the use of murderous military violence, the War on Terror has justified the creation of vast systems of policing, surveillance, and state intervention against suspected 'terrorists' and 'extremists'. In Britain, for instance, this has translated into a range of anti-terror legislation that criminalises not only direct participation in terrorist activities, but also the 'support', 'encouragement', and 'glorification' of terrorist activities and groups.[23]

In this context, several Palestinian factions – including Hamas and Palestinian Islamic Jihad – have been proscribed, such that 'displaying support' for them is unlawful. The threat of prosecution has enabled the British state to police the limits of Palestine solidarity, criminalising any acts which are deemed to have crossed over into 'support'. Crucially, this has the added effect of pushing those supporters who do not wish to be criminalised into demonstrating their solidarity in a language more closely aligned to the politics of the British state – supporting a two-state solution and endorsing Israel's 'right to defend itself'. Of

80 | RESISTING ERASURE

course, Britain here is representative of a larger global pattern.[24]

The racialised association of Palestinian liberation with 'terrorism' exists beyond the deployment of criminal law. It has also been used to cast doubt upon the legitimacy and motives of Palestine solidarity movements. Those in power – politicians, employers, university managers – have characterised those acting in solidarity with Palestine as 'mobs' of 'terrorist supporters', and worse. These characterisations have had real material effects: they have been used to shut down pro-Palestinian speech and protest and to publicly attack those who advocate Palestinian liberation.[25]

Of course, this kind of totalising racist language does not simply demonise Palestinians and their supporters. It also frames the portrayal of the Israeli state and acts to shift the terms of speech on Palestine. The Israeli state – as a bastion of European civilisation – is taken to be surrounded by barbarous and violent extremists. Given this, its deployment of military violence is characterised as – perhaps occasionally misguided – 'self-defence'.[26] For Palestine activists, this racialised narrative creates pressure to adopt a language of 'balance', in which the structural realities of colonial power are cast aside. Activists are called upon to avoid politics, stick to international law, denounce violence, and support Israel's 'right to exist' and 'right to self-defence', along with a 'two-state solution'.

The Israeli state's own racialised narrative about its position in the world is also reproduced in the Western media. This is clearly shown in the reporting of deaths. On the most basic level, the vast disparity in deaths on each side is rarely acknowledged, as this might cast doubt upon the Israeli state's assertion of self-defence. The idea that the Israeli state might intend the mass murder or ethnic cleansing of Palestinians cannot be contemplated. Moreover, in part owing to a discourse of technological advancement, any deaths that result from Palestinian violence are necessarily intended; by contrast, the deaths caused by the Israeli state are simply 'collateral damage'. We can further note that in breakdowns of Israeli deaths, rarely are women and children counted separately: the assumption is that *all* Israelis not in uniform are innocent civilians. By contrast, Palestinian deaths are frequently disaggregated to mark the number of women and children killed. While we might see this as highlighting the cruelty of the Israeli state, it should be noted that it mirrors the racial logic of the War on Terror: all adult, racialised men are potential terrorists.

Bread-and-Butter Racism

We have now seen how racism operates domestically both to delegitimise Palestine solidarity action – through aligning said action with racialised notions of terrorism – and to shore up the Israeli state, by casting it as a champion of civilised values acting in self-defence. Such characterisations operate both coercively, through the law, and ideologically, via the media. In these instances, the deployment of racism is relatively direct. The racism lies in how the Israeli state, or the Palestinian people, are presented. However, there are other, more insidious, forms of racism at play, which can be just as destructive as these direct forms.

Specifically, we refer here to the idea that acting in solidarity with Palestine is strange, eccentric, or a distraction from the real issues. This kind of 'bread-and-butter' politics is often encountered in the trade union movement, where we are told that to support the struggles of those outside the immediate workplace is too divisive, and weakens our ability to defend workers on the day-to-day matters of wages and working conditions.

Beyond unions, this framing – that Palestine is a secondary issue, distracting from the core concerns of collective organisations on the left – has been deployed across the world to stifle solidarity efforts. From academic associations arguing that Palestine falls outside their remit, to governments blocking local divestment campaigns, to universities refusing to take a stance, the argument is pervasive throughout many different spaces.[27]

Leaving aside the question of Palestine for the moment, this approach is wrong because it frames international solidarity as an act of charity, rather than a struggle that can strengthen the power of working people to organise collectively within and across borders. By campaigning and deepening awareness of how capitalism operates globally, we gain a greater understanding of how capitalism works at home. Historically, anti-colonial struggles have been inseparable from the development of anti-racist and left-wing movements in the imperialist countries – and this mutually dependent relationship has worked in both directions. To set up a dichotomy between freedom abroad and freedom at home is to weaken all of us.

In the case of Palestine, we have seen how Israeli settler colonialism is not just a localised project, but a fundamental pillar of the wider structures of American global capitalist power and our fossil-fuel-centred world. We have explored how the racialised logics that justify Israel's relentless violence are not unique – they operate globally, serving to repress and discipline other racialised communities across the world. To stand with Palestine, then, is not merely an act of solidarity with a remote and unconnected struggle somewhere far away; it is a stance against the broader structures of domination that sustain exploitation and oppression at home and abroad.

Moreover, when solidarity with Palestine is framed as divisive or 'too political', what is really being argued is that the lives and struggles of racialised people outside the West do not belong at the centre of political and labour movements. This attitude treats the concerns of certain workers – those who are predominantly white or in the Global North – as the 'real' working-class issues, while marginalising those of others. Bread-and-butter racism is not just about what is opposed but also about what is excluded. It is itself a racialising logic.

For Anti-Racist Solidarity

What we see, then, is that while Palestine cannot be understood as a simple, timeless, 'racial' clash, anti-Palestinian racism has been centrally embedded in the oppression, exploitation, and management of Palestinians. It is crucial to how Israeli settler colonialism, and the wider projects of capitalist accumulation in the region, function. Such racism underpinned the establishment of the state of Israel to begin with, and remains entwined with the very nature of the Israeli state as an ethnonationalist project. It has involved a racialised notion of security, most concretely translated into the language of terrorism. Many of the unfolding moments of imperial domination in the region have been shaped and justified through the same racial logics as those to which Palestinians have been subjected by the Israeli state. It has also proved important – in a myriad of ways – in delegitimising Palestinian solidarity and legitimising the Israeli state in the domestic context.

What, then, does all this mean for anti-racist politics more generally? Firstly, that Palestine is absolutely an anti-racist issue. Secondly, and vitally, Palestine solidarity work in this regard does not *compete* with other anti-racist movements. The basis for solidarity here is clear: anti-Palestinian racism is generated by the same set of social forces that produce other racisms; they are a connected struggle. Indeed, in a literal sense the technologies and arguments developed to police and discipline the Palestinians are *also* deployed against other racialised groups – the grim reality of the War on Terror bears this out. The tools used against Palestinians – including military technologies, surveillance, and legal frameworks – are the same mechanisms that have been deployed to marginalise racialised, Indigenous, and migrant communities across the globe.

This does not mean that all anti-racist struggles are identical; each has its own history, contradictions, and context. Movements must thoughtfully consider how to work through these in order to support and learn from one another. As the historian Robin D. G. Kelley notes, 'solidarity is not a market exchange.' It stems from a deep understanding of injustice and the systemic nature of oppression, rather than from transactional or moralistic motivations. Real solidarity comes from understanding the systems that create injustice, and building against those systems in ways that strengthen us all.

4

Against Normalisation and Erasure

It is in collectivities that we find reservoirs of hope and optimism.
   Angela Y. Davis, *Freedom Is a Constant Struggle*

We cultivate hope.
   Mahmoud Darwish, *State of Siege*

The past two decades have witnessed profound political change across the Middle East. Even before the genocide in Gaza began, the region was the most conflict-affected in the world, marked by the biggest displacement of people within and across borders.[1] The scale of human displacement in the region exists alongside its extreme wealth disparities: by 2020, some studies put the Middle East as the most unequal of any area in the world, with thirty-one billionaires holding the same amount of wealth as the bottom half of the entire adult population.[2] Such massive inequalities, combined with a long history of authoritarian rule and recurrent capitalist crises, have

88 | RESISTING ERASURE

fuelled two cycles of region-wide uprisings, in 2011 and 2018. A decade of political upheaval has followed these revolts, defined by ever-more violent state repression, armed conflict, and further waves of mass displacement.

These crises have reshaped the region's internal political landscape and also reflect a deep-seated fracturing of American hegemony in the region. Beginning in the wake of the US invasion of Iraq in 2003, many of the established pillars of US influence have eroded, and a bevy of other political forces have emerged that jostle to project their own influence. Regionally, states such as Iran, Turkey, Qatar, Saudi Arabia, and the UAE have significantly expanded their footprint, in part through the sponsorship of various armed groups and other political movements. External powers like Russia and China also play a more prominent role in the region's politics. While there is no other 'Great Power' immediately capable of displacing American influence – especially its unrivalled military strength – Washington now faces a region where its dominance is increasingly contested.

This erosion of American dominance in the Middle East is not just a regional phenomenon, but closely tied to a reconfiguration of global capitalism, and with it, global power relations. Of course, most important here has been the emergence of China and the wider East Asia region as rival zones of capital accumulation, industrial production, and financial strength. The Middle East has been pivotal to this eastward shift of the world market: the region's energy supplies are the lifeblood of China's economy, and today the great majority of the Middle East's oil and gas exports flow eastwards, rather than towards Western countries. Beyond energy, a range of other economic interdependencies now link the Middle East, China and East Asia, spanning finance, 'green' technologies, AI, construction, and infrastructure investment.[3]

Against this backdrop, American policy in the Middle East has doubled down on the strategic orientation we outlined earlier: integrating Israel more fully into the broader regional order by deepening its political and economic ties with Arab states, especially Saudi Arabia and the other Gulf monarchies. This renewed impetus for normalisation is not about diplomacy alone – it is about consolidating the region's primary centres of wealth and power within a single bloc aligned with US interests. It is through this process of normalisation that the US seeks to reassert American primacy in the region.

The Push to Normalisation

A clear indication of this strategic orientation came with the Trump-backed 2020 Abraham Accords, which saw the UAE and Bahrain formally normalise relations with Israel. This agreement, driven by significant American incentives, paved the way for a UAE–Israel free trade agreement in 2022 – the first of its kind between Israel and an Arab state. Trade between the two nations soared from just $150 million in 2020 to over $2.5 billion in 2022. Sudan and Morocco soon followed, giving Israel formal diplomatic relationships with four Arab states.[4] Today, Israel has formal relations with countries representing around 40 per cent of the Arab region's population, including some of its biggest political and economic powers.

With the inclusion of the UAE, the Abraham Accords broke the longstanding taboo on formal relationships between Israel and the Gulf states. But the UAE's importance to this process is much more than symbolic. As the leading financial centre in the Middle East, the UAE is the headquarters of many of the region's largest banks, and its economic zones sit at the core of inter-regional investment flows that will now include Israeli finance capital. The UAE is also a leading global logistics and infrastructure hub: Dubai International Airport is one of the busiest in the world, and the country runs a leading global port operator, DP World.[5]

The UAE's financial and logistical capacities make the country a key enabler of the normalisation push. This was confirmed in September 2023 with the announcement of the India–Middle East–Europe Economic Corridor (IMEC), an EU-sponsored initiative that was also backed by the US. IMEC envisions a trade and transportation network linking India to Europe through the UAE, Saudi Arabia, Israel, and Greece. Though still in its early stages, the project has advanced despite Israel's onslaught on Gaza. Indeed, during the height of Israel's bombardment, the Indian Prime Minister Narendra Modi travelled to Abu Dhabi to sign an agreement with President Mohamed bin Zayed Al Nahyan of the UAE, laying out the basic framework of IMEC. For Brussels and Washington, this represents much more than an infrastructure project: by embedding Israel within regional trade networks, IMEC is explicitly framed as a direct challenge to China's Belt and Road Initiative.[6]

Israeli political and economic leaders fully share these goals of normalisation via regional economic integration. This became evident in May 2024, when, even as Israel bombed Gaza, Netanyahu unveiled his 'Gaza 2035' plan. The plan proposed transforming Gaza into a regional economic hub, integrating it into the Israeli and Egyptian economies through the 'Gaza–Arish–Sderot Free Trade Zone'. The vision included railways, pipelines, and trade routes linking Gaza to global markets. It even presented the enclave as a future centre for electric vehicle manufacturing, where cheap Palestinian labour would produce for global supply chains (including IMEC). Within this vision, Netanyahu presented Gaza as a 'blank slate' – a territory to be 'rebuilt from scratch', as if Palestinian life, history, and resistance could simply be erased and replaced with a free trade hub.[7] According to Netanyahu, this model might be replicated in other conflict-riven states, such as Yemen, Syria, and Lebanon.

Much like the 1990s claims around Gaza becoming a

'Singapore on the Sea', the Gaza 2035 plan is a nonsensical fiction that largely serves to hide the scorched-earth destruction of Israel's war machine. But what is important here is not so much whether these plans match reality, but how they work ideologically – projecting a vision of the future in which Israel is integrated into the regional economy, and Palestinians in Gaza become a pool of cheap labour jointly exploited by both Israeli *and* Arab investors. All of this confirms the ways in which war and conflict can serve as handmaidens of capitalist expansion.

Yet, one outstanding question remains: when will Saudi Arabia agree to normalise its relations with Israel? While Riyadh undoubtedly gave its tacit approval for the UAE and Bahrain to move forward with the Abraham Accords, it has so far refrained from formal recognition of Israel – and this despite a plethora of meetings and informal connections between the two states prior to the war in Gaza. The war put these discussions on hold (at least publicly). But in the wake of Donald Trump's election, the push to normalisation has returned front-and-centre to the politics of the current moment.

Paths to Erasure and the Fictions of 'Sovereignty'

Of course, the prime obstacle to this US-led project of normalisation is the ongoing resistance of the Palestinian people, who remain overwhelmingly opposed to such initiatives. These objections are not new – they date back to the early history of Palestinian politics, when the idea of *tatbee'* (تطبيع), meaning normalisation in Arabic, was firmly rejected, and slogans like *la lil-tatbee'* (لا للتطبيع) ('no to normalisation') became a common refrain across the region, reflecting a broader principle of the movement. Because of this rejection, there is an indelible link between the imperial-sponsored politics of normalisation and the attempt to liquidate the Palestinian struggle.

At the heart of this attempted erasure is the question of Palestinian refugees and their right to return to their homes and lands from which they were expelled nearly eight decades ago. The idea of return is much more than an appeal to memory or nostalgia – it is a political demand, which directly confronts the very underpinnings of settler colonialism as a process of permanent uprooting and dispossession.

This is precisely why normalisation depends upon severing the fight for return from Palestinian politics, reducing refugees to a humanitarian issue that can be solved as part of 'final status negotiations'.

We can see this at work on multiple levels. One is the renewed push to defund and shut down the United Nations Relief and Works Agency (UNRWA), an organisation which has provided education, healthcare, and social services to Palestinian refugees since 1949. Eliminating UNRWA goes far beyond bureaucratic restructuring; it is an attempt to redefine millions of Palestinian refugees as so-called economic migrants, stripping them of their right to return, and recasting the challenge facing them as one of 'absorption' in neighbouring countries.

Another path to erasure has been the Oslo strategy, limiting the question of Palestine to promises of territorial sovereignty – promises that amount to fragmented self-rule across scattered enclaves in the West Bank and Gaza, with the exclusion of refugees and the vast majority of the Palestinian people. This playbook is drawn straight from the Bantustans of South African apartheid and the 'Indian Reserves' of Canadian settler colonialism. It is a strategy ultimately aimed at cultivating a Palestinian political leadership that is willing to give a green light to other Arab states for the normalisation project.

It is no coincidence that Saudi Arabia has openly signalled its readiness to normalise with Israel – so long as it comes with the symbolic concession of a 'Palestinian state'. Even Algeria – long a vocal supporter of the Palestinian cause – has shifted in this direction, with its president announcing in early February 2025 his support for normalisation in exchange for some kind of Palestinian statehood.

As with the Oslo years, all of this highlights the dangerous illusions embedded in the concept of 'Palestinian sovereignty'. Such rhetorical gestures are fictional and performative; they have nothing to do with the fulfilment of Palestinian rights. Their goal is to erase Palestinian history, identity, and struggle – opening up the political legitimacy for Israel's integration into the region.[8] We should do well to remember the continuities between Oslo and the genocide in Gaza. Israeli strategy has always alternated between the periodic use of extreme violence and US-sponsored negotiations – not as opposing forces, but as two sides of a single, continuous process of dispossession.

Freedom Is Global

The past seventy-six years have repeatedly shown that these efforts to permanently erase Palestinian steadfastness and resistance will fail. Despite the decades of fragmentation, a common identity and shared national experience continue to unite Palestinians – whether refugees, Palestinian citizens of Israel, or those in the West Bank, Gaza and Jerusalem. Yet, while acknowledging the ongoing reality of dispossession, we must recognise that it has also been accompanied by the emergence of new social layers and class fractions in Palestinian society, alongside varying kinds of integration into Israeli capitalism. Understanding how these political and economic logics shape the Palestinian experience today is essential for any serious liberation strategy.

With this in mind, the preceding chapters have presented an alternative perspective to the dominant ways that Palestine is typically understood – whether a focus on supposedly interminable religious conflict, Israel's massive human rights violations, or appeals to the neutrality of the international legal regime.

96 | RESISTING ERASURE

These kinds of framings serve only to depoliticise and confuse. They make it difficult to build effective solidarity, because Palestine is treated simply as a moral imperative or an exception – something that stands apart from the bigger structures of global capitalism.

In contrast to these approaches, we have instead emphasised the basic link between the dispossession of Palestinians and the politics of the wider Middle East region. Such an approach posits the struggle for Palestinian liberation not only as a confrontation with Israel, but also a challenge to the broader architecture of regional power. This is why Palestine has always been so fundamental to political movements across the Middle East. And, conversely, it is why the fate of Palestine is intimately bound up with the successes (and setbacks) of other struggles in the region.

These regional dynamics are a result of the Middle East's pivotal role in our oil-centred, capitalist world. The Gulf states, in close partnership with Western oil giants, are doubling down on hydrocarbon production, locking the planet into a trajectory of certain climate catastrophe. For the US, this deepening fossil fuel expansion – tied to its strategic alliance with the Gulf monarchies and their normalisation with Israel – is a crucial source of power at a time when American global dominance faces mounting challenges. There can be no dismantling of the fossil order, nor any genuine Palestinian liberation, without breaking apart these alliances. This is why Palestine is at its core a struggle against fossil capitalism – and why the extraordinary battle for survival waged by Palestinians today, in Gaza and beyond, is inseparable from the fight for the future of the planet.

Notes

Introduction

1 H. Abu Nada, *I Grant You Refuge* (10 October 2023), trans. H. Fakhreddine. Abu Nada was killed in an Israeli raid on Gaza on 20 October 2023, aged thirty-two.

2 A study published in the *Lancet* estimated that two in every five casualties were likely unrecorded, meaning that the actual number of deaths is much higher. R. Khatib, M. McKee, and S. Yusuf, 'Counting the Dead in Gaza: Difficult but Essential', *Lancet*, 404(10449), 2024, pp. 237–8.

3 S. Zhang, 'Gaza has highest number of child amputees per capita in the world, UN says', *Truthout*, 3 December 2024.

4 K. Hearst, 'War on Gaza: Israeli Commander Vows to Flatten "Entire" Gaza Strip', *Middle East Eye*, 21 December 2023.

5 R. Ziadah, 'Genocide, Neutrality and the University Sector', *Sociological Review*, 73(2), 2025, pp. 241–8.

6 N. Sultany, 'The Question of Palestine as a Litmus Test: On Human Rights and Root Causes', *Palestine Yearbook of International Law*, 23, 2023, pp. 9–55.

7 T. Krever et al., 'On International Law and Gaza: Critical Reflections', *London Review of International Law*, 12 (2), 2024, pp. 217, 224–5.

100 | NOTES FOR PAGES 8–13

8 For an analysis of Israel's self-definition, see M. Masri, *The Dynamics of Exclusionary Constitutionalism: Israel as a Jewish and Democratic State*, Hart Publishing, 2017.

9 See S. Englert, *Settler Colonialism: An Introduction*, Pluto Press, London, 2022. O. J. Salamanca, M. Qato, K. Rabie, and S. Samour, 'Past is Present: Settler Colonialism in Palestine', *Settler Colonial Studies*, 2(1), 2012, pp. 1–8. B. Bhandar and R. Ziadah, 'Acts and Omissions: Framing Settler Colonialism in Palestine Studies', *Jadaliyya*, 14 January 2016.

10 K. Nkrumah, 'Address at the First Seminar at the Winneba Ideological School', *Revolutionary Path*, Panaf, 1973, p. 172.

11 R. J. C. Young, *Postcolonialism: An Historical Introduction*, Blackwell, 2001, pp. 15–24.

12 In the case of Israel, much of the Western left failed to understand this point in the early decades of state build-ing, viewing the dominance of the Israeli Labour Party and the Israeli trade union federation, the Histadrut – as well as forms of colonisation such as the Kibbutzim – as evidence of 'socialism'.

13 A. Emmanuel, 'White-Settler Colonialism and the Myth of Investment Imperialism', *New Left Review*, 35, 1972.

14 F. Fanon, *Toward the African Revolution: Political Essays*, trans. H. Chevalier, Grove Press, 1988. A. Y. Davis, *Women, Race and Class*, Vintage, 1983. R. W. Gilmore, *Golden Gulag: Prisons, Surplus, Crisis, and Opposition in Globalizing California*, University of California Press, 2007. S. Hall, *Selected Writings on Race and Difference*, in P. Gilroy and R. W. Gilmore (eds), Duke University Press, 2021. A. Sivanandan, 'Race, Class and the State: The Black Experience in Britain', *Race and Class*, 17 (4), 1976, p. 347. E. Williams, *Capitalism and Slavery*, University of North Carolina Press, 1944.

NOTES FOR PAGES 13–21 | 101

15 K. E. Fields and B. J. Fields, *Racecraft: The Soul of Inequality in American Life*, reprint edition, Verso, 2014, pp. 16–17.

16 R. W. Gilmore, 'Fatal Couplings of Power and Difference: Notes on Racism and Geography', *Professional Geographer*, 54(1), 2002, p. 15.

17 W. Rodney, *How Europe Underdeveloped Africa*, Howard University Press, 1982, p. 88.

18 R. Knox, 'Valuing Race? Stretched Marxism and the Logic of Imperialism', *London Review of International Law*, 4(1), 2016, p. 81.

19 For some contemporary accounts see D. Camfield, 'Elements of a Historical-Materialist Theory of Racism', *Historical Materialism*, 24 (1), 2016, p. 31. R. Knox and A. Kumar, 'Reexamining Race and Capitalism in the Marxist Tradition – Editorial Introduction', *Historical Materialism*, 31(2), 2023. S. Virdee, *Racism, Class and the Racialized Outsider*, Bloomsbury Publishing, 2014.

1. Fossil Capitalism and Empire in the Middle East

1 Parts of this chapter are adapted from A. Hanieh, 'Framing Palestine: Israel, the Gulf States, and American Power in the Middle East', 13 June 2024. Available at: TNI.org.

2 R. J. Ortiz, 'Oil-Fueled Accumulation in Late Capitalism: Energy, Uneven Development, and Climate Crisis', *Critical Historical Studies*, 7(2), Fall 2020, pp. 205–40, 236.

3 S. Pirani, *Burning Up: A Global History of Fossil Fuel Consumption*, Pluto Press, 2018, p. 64.

4 S. Ikeda, 'World Production', in Terence Hopkins and Immanuel Wallerstein (eds), *The Age of Transition: Trajectory of the World-System, 1945–2025*, Zed Books, 1996, p. 74.

102 | NOTES FOR PAGES 21–32

5 N. Kokxhoorn, *Oil and Politics: The Domestic Roots of US Expansion in the Middle East*, Peter Lang, 1977, p. 123.

6 Ibid., p. 127.

7 A. Sampson, *The Seven Sisters: The Great Oil Companies and the World They Shaped*, Viking, 1975.

8 N. Fuccaro, 'Oilmen, Petroleum Arabism and OPEC: New Political and Public Cultures of Oil in the Arab World, 1959–1964', in Dag Harald Claes and Giuliano Garavini (eds), *Handbook of OPEC and the Global Energy Order: Past, Present and Future Challenges*, Routledge, 2020, pp. 15–30.

9 D. Eisenhower, 'Special Message to the Congress on the Situation in the Middle East', 5 January 1957, in G. Peters and J. T. Woolley (eds), *The American Presidency Project*, presidency.ucsb.edu.

10 G. Kilander, 'How much money does the US give to Israel, and is there more to come?', *Independent*, 1 November 2023. Available at: Independent.co.uk.

11 The other five countries are Ukraine, Iraq, Jordan, Tunisia, and Egypt.

12 International Jewish Anti-Zionist Network, *Israel's Worldwide Role in Repression*, 2012.

13 H. O'Dell, 'How the US has used its power in the UN to support Israel for decades', *The Chicago Council on Global Affairs*, 18 December 2023.

14 M. Dejevsky, 'Cameron's freebie to apartheid South Africa', *Independent*, 26 April 2009.

15 G. Garavini, *The Rise and Fall of OPEC in the Twentieth Century*, Oxford University Press, 2019.

16 See A. Hanieh, *Crude Capitalism: Oil, Corporate Power, and the Making of the World Market*, Verso Books, 2024.

17 T. G. Jones, 'America, Oil, and War in the Middle East', *Journal of American History*, 99(1), 2012, pp. 208–18, 215.

2. Palestinian Politics and the Oslo Accords

1. R. Khalidi, *The Hundred Years' War on Palestine: A History of Settler Colonialism and Resistance, 1917–2017*, Metropolitan Books, 2020. N. Masalha, *Palestine: A Four Thousand Year History*, Zed Books, London, 2018. R. Sayigh, *The Palestinians: From Peasants to Revolutionaries – A People's History*, Zed Books, 1979.

2. The Canadian Indian Act (1876) codified in law the separate legal status of 'Indians' and Canadian citizens, establishing reserves and a permit system. This system was directly transferred to 1950s South African apartheid. The Act also restricted Indigenous trade and enabled the removal of children to missionary schools. Dan Smith, *The Seventh Fire: The Struggle for Aboriginal Government*, Key Porter Books, 1993.

3. Between 1948 and 1967, the West Bank was ruled by Jordan and the Gaza Strip by Egypt.

4. This rule by military law was based on a similar system that had applied to Palestinian citizens of Israel until 1966. A. H. Sa'di, 'Stifling Surveillance: Israel's Surveillance and Control of the Palestinians during the Military Government Era', *Jerusalem Quarterly*, 68, 2016.

5. These expulsions were concentrated in the key agricultural area of the West Bank, the Jordan Valley, as well as a ring of villages around Jerusalem.

6. A. Samara, *The Political Economy of the West Bank 1967–1987: From Peripheralization to Development*, Khamsin Publications, London, 1988, p. 88.

7. Palestinians employed by the Village Leagues could carry weapons and arrest and interrogate people; they also dispensed permits and licenses. Many essential tasks were impossible to accomplish without Village League consent, which ultimately depended upon obeisance to the Israeli military. Funds from the Israeli government for

104 | NOTES FOR PAGES 40–2

'development' projects were channelled through the Village Leagues in an attempt to undercut support for other bodies affiliated to the PLO.

8 N. Lewin-Epstein and M. Semyonov, 'Occupational Change in Israel: Bringing the Labor Market Back', *Israel Social Science Research*, 2(2), 1984, pp. 3–18.

9 L. Farsakh, *Palestinian Labour Migration to Israel: Labour, Land and Occupation*, Routledge, 2005, pp. 82 and 217.

10 In 1970, only 43% of the employed labour force in the West Bank was comprised of wage earners. By 1987 this had increased to 63%. Money from Palestinians employed in Israel represented around one-quarter of Palestinian GNP in the West Bank and Gaza Strip between 1975 and 1985. Farsakh, *Palestinian Labour Migration*, pp. 88 and 40.

11 I. Shikaki, 'The Political Economy of Dependency and Class Formation in the Occupied Palestinian Territories Since 1967', in A. Tartir, T. Dana and T. Seidel (eds), *Political Economy of Palestine: Critical, Interdisciplinary, and Decolonial Perspectives*, Springer, 2021.

12 Fatah, led for most of its history by Yasser Arafat, continues to be the leading political force in the PLO and the Palestinian Authority, and led the negotiation of the Oslo Accords (see following). The PFLP and DFLP are the main factions of the left in the PLO. The Palestinian Communist Party, now known as the Palestinian People's Party, joined the PLO in 1987. For an overview of the complex evolution of Palestinian unions and the role of political factions through the 1970s and 1980s, see J. Hiltermann, *Behind the Intifada: Labor and Women's Movements in the Occupied Territories*, Princeton University Press, 1991, Chapter 4.

13 R. Al'Sanah, A. Hanieh and R. Ziadah, *Working Palestine: Covid-19, Labour, and Trade Unions in the West Bank and Gaza Strip*, Rosa Luxemburg Stiftung-Palestine, 2022.

NOTES FOR PAGES 42–50 | 105

14 Al-Haq, *Punishing a Nation: Human Rights Violations during the Palestinian Uprising, December 1987–1988*, Al-Haq, Ramallah, West Bank, 1989.

15 For more on movement restrictions and surveillance, see E. Zureik, D. Lyon, and Y. Abu-Laban, *Surveillance and Control in Israel/Palestine: Population, Territory, and Power*, Routledge, 2010.

16 These figures are exclusive of East Jerusalem. Areas A, B, and C now constitute around 18%, 22%, and 60% respectively of the West Bank.

17 It is not possible to delve into all the specificities of Jerusalem, including issues related to ID cards, residency rights, housing policies, access to services, and the broader impact of the Oslo Accords. See M. Nasasra, 'Occupied East Jerusalem since the Oslo Accords', in M. Turner (ed.), *From the River to the Sea: Palestine and Israel in the Shadow of 'Peace'*, Lexington Books, 2019, pp. 125–58.

18 O. J. Salamanca, 'Hooked on Electricity: The Charged Political Economy of Electrification in Palestine', in *New Direction in Palestine Studies Workshop*, Brown University, 2014.

19 H. Tawil-Souri, 'Digital Occupation: Gaza's High-Tech Enclosure', *Journal of Palestine Studies*, 41(2), 2012, pp. 27–43.

20 M. Zeitoun, *Power and Water in the Middle East: The Hidden Politics of the Palestinian–Israeli Water Conflict*, I.B. Tauris, London, 2008.

21 World Bank (2001), 'Trade Options for the Palestinian Economy', Working Paper no. 21 (English).

22 The historical lineages of this were presciently analysed in E. Farjoun, *Palestinian Workers in Israel: A Reserve Army of Labour in the Israeli Economy*, 2013. Available at: Matzpen.org.

23 For discussion of the Paris Protocol and statehood under the Palestinian Authority see: R. Khalidi and S. Samour,

'Neoliberalism as Liberation: The Statehood Program and the Remaking of the Palestinian National Movement', *Journal of Palestine Studies*, 40(2), 2011, pp. 6–25. Toufic Haddad, *Palestine Ltd: Neoliberalism and Nationalism in the Occupied Territory*, Bloomsbury Publishing, 2016.

24 S. Merrino, 'Currency and Settler Colonialism: The Palestinian Case', *Review of International Political Economy*, 28(6), 2021, pp. 1729–50.

25 'Israel to withhold $180 million in Palestinian funds over militant stipends', *Reuters*, 11 July 2021. Available at: Reuters.com.

26 Aid measured as a percentage of gross national income reached just under 50% in 2002, and has remained high since that time.

27 K. Nakhleh, 'Oslo: Replacing Liberation with Economic Neo-Colonialism', *Al-Shabaka Policy Brief*, 2014. Available at: Al-Shabaka.org.

28 K. Rabie, *Palestine Is Throwing a Party and the Whole World Is Invited: Capital and State Building in the West Bank*, Duke University Press, 2021. L. Tabar and S. Al-Botmeh, 'Real Estate Development Through Land Grabs: Predatory Accumulation and Precarity in Palestine', *New Political Economy*, 26(5), 2021, pp. 783–96.

29 A. Hanieh, *Money, Markets, and Monarchies: The Gulf Cooperation Council and the Political Economy of the Contemporary Middle East*, Cambridge University Press, 2018, Chapter 5.

30 Secondary boycotts meant that a firm invested in Israel would face exclusion from Arab markets.

31 Hashemite Kingdom of Jordan, Foreign Ministry, Middle East and North African Summits, available at: mfa.gov.jo.

32 W. Hazbun, *Beaches, Ruins, Resorts: The Politics of Tourism in the Arab World*, University of Minnesota Press, 2008, p. 116.

NOTS FOR PAGES 56–60 | 107

33 US Embassy of Israel, *Text of Cairo Conference Declaration*, 14 November 1996. Available at: Embassy-Israel.org.il.

34 A. Hanieh, *Lineages of Revolt: Issues of Contemporary Capitalism in the Middle East*, Haymarket Books, 2013, especially pp. 36–8.

35 Palestinian political prisoners are a cornerstone of the broader Palestinian struggle; their release is a powerful rallying cry within the national movement. See R. Qatamish and N. Sha'ban, *Torture of Palestinian Political Prisoners in Israeli Prisons*, trans. by Diab Zayed, Addameer Prisoners Support and Human Rights Association, 2003.

36 After Israel's establishment in 1948, Palestinian citizens of Israel endured military rule until 1966, which shaped subsequent policies in the West Bank and Gaza. Economically marginalised, they face poverty, high unemployment, and restricted resources, worsened by increased surveillance and state violence. See N. N. Rouhana and A. Sabbagh-Khoury, 'Settler-Colonial Citizenship: Conseptualizing the Relationship between Israel and Its Palestinian Citizens', *Settler Colonial Studies*, 5(3), 2015, pp. 205–25.

37 D. Li, 'The Gaza Strip as Laboratory: Notes in the Wake of Disengagement', *Journal of Palestine Studies*, 35(2), 2006, pp. 38–55.

38 After the death of Yasser Arafat in 2004, Mahmoud Abbas took over leadership of the PA and the main PLO political faction, Fatah. Elections for the Palestinian Legislative Council (PLC), held in January 2006, saw a massive swing towards Hamas (winning 74 out of the 132 seats). Initially, a national unity government was formed between Hamas and Fatah, but this was dissolved by Abbas after Hamas seized control of the Gaza Strip on 14 June 2007. The complete separation of the two territories was sealed by an unprecedented Israeli blockade of Gaza that began from that moment.

NOTES FOR PAGES 60–7

39 R. Smith, 'Israel's Permanent Siege of Gaza', *Middle East Report*, 290, Spring 2019, pp. 38–42.

40 United Nations Relief and Works Agency for Palestine Refugees in the Near East (UNRWA), 'Gaza Strip: Socio-Economic Snapshot – 2022', 2022.

41 Palestinians in Gaza have repeatedly attempted to break through this economic strangulation. An important example was the 2019 mass mobilisation staged near the Gaza–Israel border, with participants setting up camps and demanding justice, self-determination, and the right of return of refugees. The Israeli military responded using live ammunition, tear gas, and sniper fire, resulting in the deaths of hundreds and injuries to thousands, many of them young people. J. Abusalim, 'What is "The Great Return March?"', American Friends Services Committee Blog, 19 April 2019.

42 S. Seikaly, 'Counting Calories and Making Lemonade in Gaza', *Jadaliyya*, 12 November 2019.

3. Racialising Palestine

1 R. Knox, 'International Law, Race, and Capitalism: A Marxist Perspective', *AJIL Unbound*, 117, 2023, p. 55.

2 A. Anghie, *Imperialism, Sovereignty, and the Making of International Law*, Cambridge University Press, 2005, pp. 32–114. For approaches centring capitalism, see R. Knox, 'Imperialism, Hypocrisy and the Politics of International Law', *Third World Approaches to International Law Review*, 2022, pp. 25, 47–51; N. Tzouvala, *Capitalism As Civilisation: A History of International Law*, Cambridge University Press, 2020, pp. 1–88.

3 M. Craven, 'What Happened to Unequal Treaties? The Continuities of Informal Empire', *Nordic Journal of International Law*, 74, 2005, p. 335.

4 J. Renton, 'Flawed Foundations: The Balfour Declaration

NOTES FOR PAGES 68–71 | 109

and the Palestine Mandate', in Rory Miller (ed.), *Britain, Palestine and Empire: The Mandate Years*, Routledge, 2010.

5 For a comprehensive account of the theorical and political underpinnings of this process both in Palestine and in the wider colonial world, see B. Bhandar, *Colonial Lives of Property: Law, Land, and Racial Regimes of Ownership*, Duke University Press, 2018.

6 See Anghie, *Imperialism, Sovereignty*, pp. 116–95.

7 See Hanieh, *Crude Capitalism*, Chapter 3, for a discussion of oil, Iran, and British colonialism.

8 Susan Pedersen notes the British claim that it would 'safeguard only the non-Jewish population's "civic and religious" and not their "political" rights' was a source of controversy, even after a 'strained claim' that civil rights would include political rights. S. Pedersen, *The Guardians: The League of Nations and the Crisis of Empire*, Oxford University Press, 2015, p. 35. Indeed, these words represented the literal incorporation of the Balfour Declaration into the Mandate: see Pedersen, 'Writing the Balfour Declaration into the Mandate for Palestine', *International History Review*, 45(2), 279, 2023.

9 As the first British colonial governor of Jerusalem famously put it, Jewish immigration to Palestine would form 'for England a little loyal Jewish Ulster in a sea of potentially hostile Arabism'. R. Storrs, *The Memoirs of Sir Ronald Storrs*, G.P. Putnam's Sons, 1937, p. 364, archive.org, viewed 4 February 2025.

10 A. Sabbagh-Khoury, *Colonizing Palestine: The Zionist Left and the Making of the Palestinian Nakba*, Stanford University Press, 2023.

11 Note, for instance, the different degrees to which Māori and Australian Aboriginal populations were able to resist British settler colonialism in the Pacific. The former deployed modern weaponry and military tactics in

110 | NOTES FOR PAGES 72–5

numerous wars against settlement between 1845 and 1872. One consequence of this resistance was a much higher survival rate for the Māori population in New Zealand in comparison to Australian indigenous populations.

12 In the 2018–19 Great March of Return, a series of peaceful demonstrations by Palestinians, the Israeli military used deadly force, claiming 'Hamas . . . was using the protests as a guise to launch attacks against Israel and ignite the area.' T. Lazaroff and Reuters, 'IDF warns of larger military response to Gaza protest', *Jerusalem Post*, 31 March 2018. Available at: JPost.com.

13 See 'Israel's Apartheid against Palestinians: A Cruel System of Domination and a Crime against Humanity', Amnesty International, 1 February 2022. O. Shakir, 'A Threshold Crossed: Israeli Authorities and the Crimes of Apartheid and Persecution', Human Rights Watch, 27 April 2021. These reports detail in an extensive manner the racialised forms of control practised systematically by the Israeli state.

14 S. R. David, 'Israel's Policy of Targeted Killing', *Ethics & International Affairs*, 17(1), 2003, p. 111.

15 M. Gunneflo, *Targeted Killing: A Legal and Political History*, Cambridge University Press, 2016.

16 Staff, 'Israel Confirms It Killed Hamas Political Chief Ismail Haniyeh in Iran in July', *Guardian*, 24 December 2024.

17 A. Loewenstein, *The Palestine Laboratory: How Israel Exports the Technology of Occupation Around the World*, 1st edition, Verso, 2023.

18 R. Knox, 'Civilizing Interventions? Race, War and International Law', *Cambridge Review of International Affairs*, 26(1), 2013, p. 111. For the ever-present sense of surveillance from drones, see: Columbia Law School Human Rights Clinic and Center for Civilians in Conflict, 'The

NOTES FOR PAGES 76–82 | 111

Civilian Impact of Drones: Unexamined Costs, Unanswered Questions', n.d. Available at: law.columbia.edu.

19 R. Parfitt, *The Process of International Legal Reproduction: Inequality, Historiography, Resistance*, Cambridge University Press, 2019, p. 43.

20 N. Tzouvala, 'TWAIL and the "Unwilling or Unable" Doctrine: Continuities and Ruptures', *AJIL Unbound*, 109, 2015, pp. 266–70.

21 N. Tzouvala, 'The "Unwilling or Unable" Doctrine and the Political Economy of the War on Terror', *Humanity: An International Journal of Human Rights, Humanitarianism, and Development*, 14(1), 2023, pp. 19–28.

22 Even in cases where this has coincided with support for Hamas – as with Qatar – this support itself has been with the permission and endorsement of the US.

23 Terrorism Act (2000); Terrorism Act (2006) s.1; Terrorism Act (2006) s.1(1).

24 See, for example: Center for Constitutional Rights and Palestine Legal, *Anti-Palestinian at the Core: The Origins and Growing Dangers of U.S. Antiterrorism Law*, February 2024. Available at: ccrjustice.org. S. Tanno, 'No European Country More than Germany Is Going Further in Clamping Down on Hamas', CNN, 28 January 2024. Available at: CNN.com.

25 'Pupils Wearing Pro-Palestinian Badges Referred to Counter-Terror Scheme – Union', *Independent*, 4 April 2024. Available at: Independent.co.uk. R. Syal, D. Sabbagh and K. Stacey, 'Suella Braverman Calls Pro-Palestine Demos "Hate Marches"', *Guardian*, 30 October 2023.

26 R. Knox, 'Against Self-Defence', Legal Form, 25 October 2024. Available at: legalform.blog.

27 A related form of this racism is the claim to neutrality, where Palestine is framed as inherently too controversial to take up at all. Often presented as pragmatism, this claim functions as an endorsement of the status quo.

4. Against Normalisation and Erasure

1 World Bank, *The Economics of Post-Conflict Reconstruction in MENA*, Washington, DC, 2017. Available at: WorldBank.org.

2 ESCWA, *The Impact of COVID-19 on the Arab Region: An Opportunity to Build Back Better*, Policy Brief, Beirut, Economic and Social Commission for Western Asia, 2020. Available at: UN.org.

3 Hanieh, *Crude Capitalism*, Chapter 12.

4 In the case of Sudan, the US agreed to provide a $1.2 billion loan and to remove the country from its list of state sponsors of terrorism (although the final normalisation agreement remains unratified). For Morocco, the US recognised Moroccan sovereignty over Western Sahara in return for the country's normalisation with Israel.

5 R. Ziadah, 'Transport Infrastructure and Logistics in the Making of Dubai Inc.', *International Journal of Urban and Regional Research*, 42(2), 2018, pp. 182–97.

6 A. Cornwell and B. M. Kamdar, 'India, UAE sign pact on trans-continental trade corridor', Reuters, 14 February 2024. Available at: Reuters.com.

7 K. Wagner, 'The Awful Plan to Turn Gaza into the Next Dubai', *The Nation*, 9 July 2024. Available at: TheNation.com.

8 Often the statehood won by national liberation movements in the post-war period led to their integration into a global capitalist market that preserved colonial boundaries and kept the former colonies subordinate. See M. W. Mutua, 'Why Redraw the Map of Africa: A Moral and Legal Inquiry', *Michigan Journal of International Law*, 16, 1995, p. 1113.